Tahoe Heritage

Foreword by

Robert Laxalt

University of

Nevada Press

Reno, Las Vegas,

& London

The Bliss Family of Glenbrook, Nevada

by Sessions S. Wheeler

with William W. Bliss

Tahoe
Heritage

WWB

The paper used in this book meets the requirements of American National Standard for Information Sciences — Permanence of Paper for Printed Library Materials, ANSI Z39-48.1984.

The Library of Congress has cataloged the hardcover edition as follows:

Wheeler, Sessions S.
  Tahoe heritage : the Bliss family of Glenbrook, Nevada / by Sessions S. Wheeler with William W. Bliss ; foreword by Robert Laxalt.
     p.   cm.
  Includes bibliographical references (p.   ) and index.
  ISBN 0-87417-185-7 (cloth ed. : acid-free paper)
  1. Tahoe Lake Region (Calif. and Nev.) — History. 2. Bliss family. 3. Tahoe Lake Region (Calif. and Nev.) — Biography.
I. Bliss, William W. (William Walter), 1924 –   . II. Title.
F868.T2W48   1992
979.4'38 — dc20   91-40147
                                                         CIP

ISBN 0-87417-299-3 (paperback edition)
University of Nevada Press, Reno, Nevada 89557 USA
Copyright © 1992 University of Nevada Press
All rights reserved
Printed in the United States of America
Book design by Richard Hendel

Paperback edition published in 1997
01 00 99 98 97   5 4 3 2 1

Dedicated to

the memory of

Duane, William,

and Will Bliss

Contents

Foreword : ix

Preface : xiii

One   A Man Named Diston : 1

Two   Gold Hill, Nevada, 1864 : 7

Three   Early Settler from Maine : 15

Four   Carson and Tahoe Lumber and Fluming Company : 26

Five   A Box of Letters : 39

Six   Lake Tahoe Railway and Transportation Company : 47

Seven   To Nome : 60

Eight   Letters from Nome : 71

Nine   End of an Era : 79

Ten   Tahoe Water : 86

Eleven   Time of Change : 94

Twelve   A New Direction : 104

Thirteen   Fishing : 109

Fourteen   Rodeos : 114

Fifteen   Golf and Tennis : 119

Sixteen   The Final Years : 128

Epilogue : 138

Notes : 141

Index : 149

Foreword

Sessions Wheeler and William Bliss—co-authors of this book—seem always to go together with my memories of Glenbrook. One name triggers the other in my youthful recollections of being a caddy at that green jewel of a golf course, its fairways winding through the pines of the Sierra forest on the shores of Lake Tahoe.

I remember the first time I saw Buck Wheeler. He was a man with a gentle nature and an easy ground-eating way of walking. He was not a power hitter but a straight one. This is more important at Glenbrook, where getting out of the forest rough is like playing billiards with golf balls.

Bill Bliss blends into that period of my life, slender and sun-burned and working on the Glenbrook grounds like any laborer.

Though his family owned Glenbrook, he was being raised in the Bliss tradition of working one's way up from apprenticeship to a position of authority.

In later days I knew of Buck Wheeler in another context—writer and teacher. His formative years, writing outdoor sportsman and conservation columns in newspapers and magazines, had earned him a following.

When Buck was a biology teacher at Reno High School, he had to ride herd over a windowless basement study hall that students called "the black hole of Calcutta." Buck had a choice of an hour of boredom or an hour of writing. So, from the "black hole" was to emerge his first book-length work—*Paiute*. That empathetic story of Indian life and wars in the Nevada of the 1860s has had a long and enduring life in bookstores since it was first published in 1963.

In the years since, five more books of enduring value have undergone the transition from handwritten script to the printed page. Heart and mind and meticulous research emanate from each one of those printed pages.

"The *how* I work on a book is influenced by a realization that I could never make a living from writing," Buck was to write in a magazine profile. "What I have going for me is a strong desire to write, persistence, a fear of writing poorly, some ability to critically judge what I've written . . . and a mysterious sort of aid which most people call the subconscious." One of his pet peeves is, as he puts it, "the vast amount of inaccurate history which careless research preserves generation after generation."

It was in this vital field of research that coauthor Bill Bliss was to figure. Private Bliss family journals, letters, photos, and Bill Bliss's own recollections of unrecorded facts filled the well that is the heart core of *Tahoe Heritage*.

Hostelries have long been an accepted genre of historical research and writing. Glenbrook qualifies in the best of ways. Here, we have a history of an inn from its earliest days in the 1860s to its closing in 1976. We see Glenbrook's sturdy but genteel climb to its peak as a hostelry for the elite of San Francisco and California. We witness Glenbrook's tenacity in warding off the temptations of gambling casinos. We find an added surprise—a nautical history of Lake Tahoe from timbering barges to passenger steamers.

Even more importantly, we have a chronicle of a remarkable family of larger-than-life figures with their roots sunk deep into living western history. The story is told with a sympathy unusual to most histories, obviously because the authors' lives were so inter-mingled with the story of Glenbrook.

Robert Laxalt

Preface

Duane L. Bliss was one of Nevada's eminent pioneers. During the momentous days of the Comstock Lode he helped to make it possible for other men to break into the desert mountains' great underground treasure vaults where, over millions of years, Nature had stored thousands of tons of silver and gold. He was highly respected for his integrity, honesty, and ability by the hundreds of men who worked for him, by the early residents who knew him, and by the politicians whose names went down in the history books.

But in more recent years, aside from those who have visited the beautiful Lake Tahoe park which bears the name "D. L. Bliss State Park," few current Nevadans or tourists have ever heard of him, and most of the books which mention his name devote little more than a line or a paragraph to it.

During an evening in June of 1989, while working on a new book, I wondered why I had not attempted to write a history of the Bliss family. I had enough sketchy knowledge of the subject and some personal experience with various members of the family to feel there might be the necessary ingredients for an interesting story, one that hopefully would provide a small addition to Nevada history. I also knew a possible source of accurate information.

After the death of his father in 1960, William W. "Bill" Bliss was the operating owner of the Glenbrook Inn at Lake Tahoe until its closing in 1976, and I wondered if he had memories, passed down through three generations of his family, of the part Duane Bliss and his family had played in the story of the Comstock Lode and Lake Tahoe.

I met with Bill the next day and learned that he had stored away several boxes of family letters, many old and new photographs, and other documents. We agreed to work together, that Bill would provide information unavailable elsewhere, photographs, and discussions of modern events, and I would do the research and writing. Without Bill Bliss's invaluable aid, most of the story could not have been told.

The book is neither written as nor intended to be biographical in nature. Instead its purpose is the same as most of my other books— to gather the interesting history of a region and make it more readily available to readers who enjoy western Americana.

The story is based on historical fact. Its first chapter, which relies on a short biographical sketch by Duane Bliss's eldest son, could not be related understandably here without the addition of details based upon research and a certain amount of dialogue that clarifies the compassion a professional gambler had for a sixteen-year-old Duane Bliss—a compassion which saved the boy's life and started him on his remarkable career.

S.S.W.

ACKNOWLEDGMENTS

To tell this story, based on the Bliss family's vital materials, the writer required information and advice from professionals in various fields. Because several pages of my notes are missing, I suspect that the following list of names of those who helped the book is not complete. For that I apologize.

To Robert Laxalt, Senator Paul Laxalt, Ronald Hess, Robert Blesse, David Myrick, Lee Mortensen, Nancy Martineau, Tony Payne, Almo Cordone, Thomas Trelease, John Morrison, Gary Stone, Jeff Blyer, Richard Hardyman, Carl Dodge, Frank Titus, Winston Dinkel, Barbara Butler, and editor Nick Cady, I am grateful.

S.S.W.

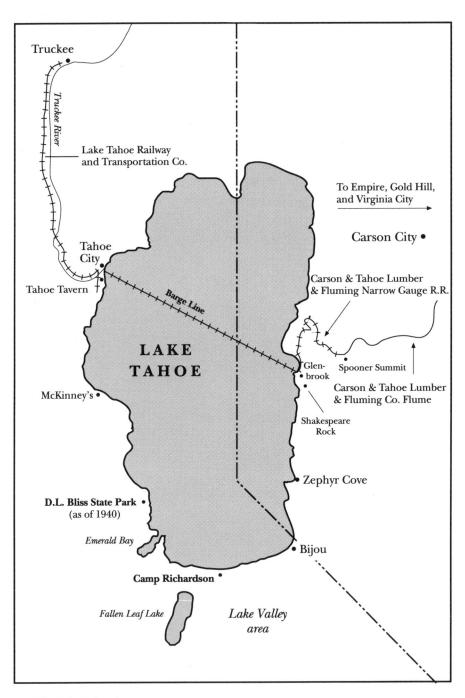

Truckee

Truckee River

Lake Tahoe Railway
and Transportation Co.

To Empire, Gold Hill,
and Virginia City ➔

Carson City •

Tahoe
City

Tahoe Tavern

Barge Line

Carson & Tahoe Lumber
& Fluming Narrow Gauge R.R.

**LAKE
TAHOE**

Glen-
brook

Spooner Summit

Carson & Tahoe Lumber
& Fluming Co. Flume

McKinney's •

Shakespeare
Rock

Zephyr Cove

D.L. Bliss State Park •
(as of 1940)

Emerald Bay

Bijou

Camp Richardson •

Fallen Leaf Lake

*Lake Valley
area*

The Lake Tahoe Area, ca. 1900.

One :
A Man
Named
Diston

More than twenty thousand 1849 emigrants were struggling across plains, mountains, and deserts toward the California gold fields when sixteen-year-old Duane Leroy Bliss decided to follow his urge for adventure and travel by ship to Panama, by foot across the isthmus, and again by sea to San Francisco.

It would not be the first adventure away from home for the son of William and Lucia Mary Bliss of Savoy, Massachusetts, an exceptionally bright boy who had completed his schooling at the age of thirteen in 1846. After his mother's death that same year, he shipped as a cabin boy on a sailing vessel for a two-year voyage to South America.[1] It was two years of learning discipline, self-reliance, and self-respect; when he returned to Savoy in 1848, he was tall, lean, and strong for his age—more a young man than a boy.

Duane spent the winter teaching in the village school[2] while gathering information about the West, where California stream-beds were said to be yielding fortunes in gold nuggets. He had saved most of his earnings from the South American trip, which, along with his teaching salary and a small inheritance from his mother, he believed would support him until he had an opportunity either to find a mining claim or to work in the gold fields for other miners. It was not until the fall of 1849 that he was able to secure passage on one of the crowded ships for the first leg of his journey.

Aboard the steamer en route to Panama he met a man named Diston.[3] It is not known how they became acquainted, but the beginning of a friendship had developed by the time the ship dropped anchor outside the mouth of the Chagres River, gateway to travel across the isthmus. Small boats manned by natives met the steamer and carried its passengers to the town of Chagres—a miserable-looking settlement on both sides of the river with a reputation for disease and numerous murders.

Although there was a small vessel propelled by a steam engine taking on passengers, Diston led the way to a larger than average flat-bottom rowboat with four oarsmen and addressed the master in Spanish. Duane had become capable in that language during the two-year South American voyage, and from the conversation he learned that they would travel upstream, aided for some distance by the tide, and would stay the night at a small, unnamed settlement. The next day they would reach a place named Gorgona, where they would leave the river to travel the remaining distance to Panama City on mules.

With baggage loaded, the boat moved up the river with seeming ease, passing between heavily forested hills covered with flowering shrubs and other plants reaching down to river banks where color-ful birds and noisy monkeys greeted them.[4] At several places they saw men at work building a railroad which Diston estimated would reduce the time required to cross the isthmus from approximately three days to about three hours.[5] The advantage of the flat-bot-tom boat became apparent when they passed a small iron steamer grounded on a sandbar.

[2]

Only primitive accommodations were available where they stopped for the night, and when they reached the Gorgona hotel the next day, they found it crowded. Rumors of bandits who might attack travelers along tomorrow's trail seemed to occupy most of the conversation among the guests.

Following a night's rest and early breakfast, Duane and Diston joined a mule train for the final twenty-two-mile ride to Panama City. The trail passed through deep, narrow gullies and in stretches was muddy and rocky, but the mules were sure-footed and along the worst of the route seemed to know where to step to avoid a hole or a loose rock. Nearing Panama City, Duane noticed that the road had been paved with stones, and Diston said that Francisco Pizarro, the conqueror of Peru, had ordered it done. Over the centuries most of the stones had been scattered or buried in mud.[6]

Diston and Duane secured rooms at the American Hotel. After getting settled and learning that a steamer was due to leave for San Francisco within the week, they had dinner together. Diston had several business engagements, and Duane, feeling unusually exhausted, retired.

Shortly before dawn Duane awakened with a headache and nausea. By the time Diston knocked on the door on his way to breakfast, Duane realized that he was very ill. In addition to the headache and nausea, he was suffering a high fever. The hotel manager recommended a physician who had received his training in the United States, and Diston headed for his office.

It did not take the doctor long to diagnose Duane's illness as a disease locally known as "Chagres Fever,"[7] which he said had killed hundreds of people during the past two years. He offered some hope for recovery if the patient received the proper care, which included strict bed rest in clean surroundings and nursing by someone who was experienced in taking care of Chagres Fever patients. Diston made financial arrangements with the manager which would allow the boy to remain in the hotel room until he was well.

With days turning into weeks, Duane—sometimes comatose or delirious—remained critically ill. Diston spent part of each morning and evening helping a woman keep the boy and his bed clean and feed him the liquid diet specially prepared by a restaurant. It was not until after the first of the year that the doctor was satisfied that the crisis had passed.[8]

Diston was there the first morning Duane was allowed to take a few steps around the room. The boy had awakened early thinking of the sacrifice his friend had made and how he could repay him. He had decided to use all of the money in his money-belt as partial payment of the nurse and hotel and to attempt to get a job at the hotel to pay the remainder. When he told Diston of his plan, the man smiled approval but said that all bills had been paid.

The boy started to object, but Diston explained that he was a professional gambler and a mine owner who could easily afford to pay all expenses.

Seriously weakened muscles from the long period of lying in bed responded slowly to exercises, and it was early spring before Duane was strong enough to travel. They secured passage on a ship to San Francisco, where Diston had reserved rooms in a hotel owned by a friend.

During breakfast the first morning after landing, Diston knew it was time to discuss the future. Looking at the boy he said, "I know you came out here hoping to mine gold. If you made inquiries of the men who have returned from the goldfields, you would find that a high percentage of them were unsuccessful. The streams have been worked for two years now, and most of those that are still producing are claimed.

"Today I go to Sacramento where I have a business engagement for several days. Duane, I don't intend to have you follow my profession,[9] and I am going to have to leave you. I suggest that you investigate work here; you may find something that you would enjoy. If you do not find what you want here you might try Sacramento, which may be considerably less expensive than living in San Francisco; and of more importance to you, Sacramento is the central point from which prospectors head for the mining country and to which miners return to obtain supplies and mail. You might find a miner who needs help in working his claim, which could provide a good way to get started."

As they parted Duane wished to express gratitude for everything the man had done for him, but feeling too emotional to speak, he took Diston's extended hand and turned away.

The ship slipped smoothly to a stop alongside the Sacramento wharf where heavy hawsers warped it in place, allowing passengers to begin going ashore. Duane had spent two weeks in San Francisco unsuccessfully searching for work. Now, in Sacramento, he knew he must find a job before he used more of his savings, and he set out to locate an inexpensive hotel room. He had not walked far, threading his way along the crowded main street, when he heard his name called and turned to see Diston coming toward him.[10]

Minutes later, to get free of the crowd, they were ordering coffee at a nearby restaurant, and the gambler was saying that their meeting had saved him a trip to San Francisco to try to find Duane.

That week he had bought a small claim from a man who had developed a lung ailment and wanted to get home. The man claimed he had panned several hundred dollars worth of nuggets before becoming too ill to work in the cold water. Diston gave him the money he needed, and the miner signed over his claim, drawing a map of the location.

The gambler turned to the boy. "I thought it might be a good place for you to make a few hundred dollars, or at least get mining out of your system. So if you want it, I'll take you up there day after tomorrow. First you will have to get outfitted with proper clothes, rubber boots, and a bedroll. We go by steamer to Marysville where we will pick up a couple of mules and a lot of food. Fortunately, the man's tools are stored in a small shack he built, so we don't have to worry about that. Do you want to give it a try?"

Duane didn't hesitate in accepting. Diston saw the boy's gratitude.

During the trip by steamer from Sacramento to Marysville, Diston briefed Duane on his knowledge of mining small streams, and several experienced miners volunteered additional details. A day was spent in Marysville obtaining three mules—two for riding and the third for packing. It was mid-June before they reached Diston's claim.

Duane was eager to explore the short stretch of stream which had been posted, but he set to work removing the saddles and packs from their animals which, after being hobbled, began feeding on the abundant early summer grass. The small cabin contained two shovels, a pick, several prospector's pans, some buckets, and a rocker,[11] all of which he moved outside to provide room for sleeping. In the meantime Diston had been cooking dinner over a small fire.

Later, when the sun was beginning to drop behind the canyon ridge, they examined the stream; wet banks told that the water level had recently dropped.

Diston wished to leave early the next morning, and while breakfast was being prepared he saddled his mule, tying his bedroll behind his saddle. Glancing at Duane he said he was leaving the other two animals in case Duane needed them if he moved to a new location. If he left the mining country, he could sell the mules in Marysville. He added that if anyone inquired about his ownership of the claim, to say that "Diston put you there."[12]

As Diston was leaving, Duane asked, "If this claim turns out to be very rich, is there any way I could reach you so that you could share in the profits?"

Diston shook his head, "I'm afraid not. Actually I do not know where I'll be. I may have to go to the East again. We have gotten to be close friends, Duane, and leaving is as hard on me as on you, maybe harder." Diston swung into his saddle, reaching down to take the boy's hand. When he started on his way, he did not look back. Duane watched him pass out of sight around a bend in the canyon.

Sitting quietly beside the stream, the boy thought of the past months: why had this remarkable man sacrificed so much of his time and money to aid a boy with whom he had no ties of relationship or other responsibility? To have helped obtain medical aid in Panama City would have been considered exceptional kindness. But Diston had delayed his trip for six months to take care of him, as if he was caring for his own son.

And now he had given him a mining claim, a chance to start a new way of life.

More than anything else, the boy hoped Diston knew his gratitude.

[6]

Two :
Gold Hill,
Nevada,
1864

Hoping that hard work would help overcome his loneliness for his friend, Duane began improving his camp.

Both mules seemed satisfied with the grass in the vicinity. He could hear the bells attached to their necks, so he turned his attention to cleaning the shack and patching holes in the roof. The former occupant had built a rough, outdoor stove with a piece of sheet metal supported on rocks, which Duane rearranged to make it more suitable for cooking the foods he had brought. A cupboard inside the cabin was made as moisture- and rodent-proof as possible.

That afternoon he began studying the stream and decided to begin work where a rock shelf projected out into the central current. The water was not more than two feet deep and because of the canyon's steepness was quite swift. He had been instructed to dig down to bedrock, where most nuggets would be lodged.

His first panning resulted in no sign of the gold color he had hoped to see. For his second attempt, he moved closer to the rock ledge, and as he worked the pan there was a yellow flash which, with the clearing of sediment, proved to be a nugget the size of a small bean.

It was the next day that two men came to his camp while he was preparing dinner. By their expressions, Duane guessed they were not making a friendly visit, and he was not surprised when one said, "We think you are working on someone else's land."

Duane, remembering his friend's instruction, answered, "Diston put me here."

One of the strangers looked at the other, who shrugged and said, "If Diston put you here, I guess you can stay until it is definitely decided whether this small property is part of one of the adjoining claims."

The miners' visit changed Duane's daily routine. Not knowing how long it might be before he lost the opportunity to mine the rich stream, he decided to begin working from sunrise to sunset, using the rocker with which he could handle more pay dirt each day.

Near the end of July 1850 the two miners returned to tell him that, according to the "Miner's Code,"[1] he would have to move. Realizing he had no choice but to accept the decision, he agreed to close up the camp and leave the following day.

When he packed the mules, he felt satisfied with the weight of his saddlebags. He wished there was some way Diston could know.

On reaching San Francisco, Duane's first concern was the security of the gold he carried. At the Adams Express Company, which offered banking services to miners, his gold was carefully weighed and stored in buckskin bags which were sealed, labeled, and their values entered in the company's books before being placed in a safe. Duane retained one of the bags, which contained enough gold dust to provide for his needs until he found employment.

Wishing to leave the crowded city, Duane traveled down the San

Francisco Peninsula to Woodside, where he found work at a Dr. Tripp's general store. Eventually he left there to go to Trinity Center in northern California where he acquired an interest in a combination hotel and store. The proprietor, John P. Jones, competed with other merchants for trade and managed to obtain most of it. Jones was a natural salesman who told such interesting stories that miners would stop by in the evenings to hear them and to trade.

Born in England in 1829, Jones had been brought to America by his parents when he was two years of age. The family settled in Cleveland, where Jones received a common school education before working as a clerk in a forwarding house and a teller in the Canal Bank of Cleveland. Shortly after news of the California gold strike reached the East, he and his brother Henry set out for California on a sailing ship, the bark *Eureka* of 400 tons which, routed around Cape Horn, reached the Golden Gate nine months later.

Jones worked for a short time in the San Francisco Customs House before beginning mining in Calaveras and Tuolumne counties. In 1852 he started his public career, serving in Trinity County as justice of the peace, then deputy sheriff, then sheriff, and then state senator for four years.[2]

Jones and Bliss became close friends during the years they worked together. When they parted they could not have guessed what the future had in store for them.

b 1833

In 1860, twenty-seven-year-old Duane Bliss joined the thousands of Californians headed over the Sierras for the great Comstock Lode. He settled in Gold Hill, where his intelligence and personality were soon recognized. Before the year was out, he was hired to manage the Comstock's first quartz mill, which was built in Silver City by Almarin B. Paul.

With the funds he had brought to the West, the gold he had obtained from Diston's claim, and the sale of his interest in the Trinity Center hotel and store, Duane had enough savings to become a partner in the Gold Hill banking firm of Almarin B. Paul, Duane L. Bliss, and W. H. Baker.

J. Ross Browne, a visitor to Gold Hill and Virginia City in 1860, described the area as "frame shanties pitched together as if by accident; tents of canvas, of brush, of blankets, of potato sacks, and old shirts."[3] In 1863, Duane Bliss traveled to the East to marry Elizabeth T. Tobey of South Wareham, Massachusetts. In place of a honeymoon, he brought his bride to the Comstock area Browne had described. Elizabeth wrote her aunt a long letter which provides an interesting account of the region four years after Browne's description:

June 30, 1864

My Dear Aunt:

I remember you telling me to be sure to give you my impressions of this place. They certainly are more favorable than I expected they would be when on board the steamer. There were two gentlemen who had been there three years ago when it was but a year old, and they told me I could never live here, it was a god forsaken place, etc. etc., and Duane did not take pains to correct their statements, not caring how poor an idea I had of the place, thinking it always better to be happily surprised than otherwise. I left the coach, after traveling in it all day and night, at Carson some seventeen miles from here with as dirty a face as I ever remember since I got to be over twenty years old. After trying a half hour to make myself decent to see strangers, was presented to a young friend of Duane's who had come with Mr. Paul's teams to take us to our place of destination. At Carson we took breakfast, it being about eight o'clock, and as soon as convenient we started on our journey, finding it, however, much more comfortable in a private than public conveyance. I saw very little of note— excepting now and then a mill with a shaft sunk in the mountain by means of which the mill was supplied with ore—until we got to Silver City which is a place about the size of Rochester, but the houses are smaller.

The land is barren, producing only sagebrush except, occasionally, as handsome flowers as I ever saw. They were really beautiful. There was a species resembling portulaca very much, being white and pink blossoms on one stalk; then there was a blue flower that looked precisely like larkspur, beside a variety of others. It seemed quite strange to me that they could be contented to grow where not a spear of grass showed itself.

After leaving Silver City we soon found ourselves in Gold Hill, the entrance to which place is called the Devil's Gate and it truly looks as though he had a hand in building it. It is a mountainous pass, on either side of which are many huge rocks 120 feet high and in the most rugged shape you can imagine. Great boulders that are sticking out all over it looked as though they were just ready to fall. It is frightful but yet so grand. I have heard there were photographs of it and if I can find one will send it home so you will be able to form some idea of it. It did not take long to get through the pass and we had entered the most humble of all humble places, as I supposed, with my eyes as wide open as the dust and sleepless night would allow, to take in all its drawbacks at once. But instead [of] finding brown hills with white enormous holes dug into them where the ore was taken out and with them a miner's hut with now and then a frame building, I found a large village with the houses, most of them small cottages, just as close at the foot of the mountain on either side of the street as they could stand. Then there are streets out into the mountain and houses are built there also. For people to get up to them from the main street there are stairs in some places and in others you have to climb on paths.

The houses are furnished well and there is much more dress displayed here than on Beacon Street when the ladies make calls. They seldom walk out for pleasure. Their houses are too small to entertain company for any length of time so visiting is seldom thought of, but they call often. I have had a quantity of callers and I like them very much with but one or two exceptions. And such a display of dress I never expected to see here. They never think of wearing anything but point and thread lace. A Mrs. Winters came with her carriage to call on me yesterday and Mrs. Vesey said that her collar and sleeves must have cost one hundred dollars and the rest of her dress in comparison. She had on a thread lace cape, blue bands of silk. Cheap dress goods are not kept in the stores. And in Virginia, which is but a half a mile from here, there are better stores than in New Bedford, and I do not believe as nice silk can be found in Boston.

There are no old and but very few poor people. I have not seen a beggar except Indians since I have been here. I was in a store yesterday morning and there was an Indian woman with her papoose strapped to a board and carried on her back by means of a leather strap which she wore around her head. The board is formed like the top of a small coffin, small at the feet and large at the head. The babies are held in something that looks like a basket fastened to the board and it comes over the baby's head. The baby's

[11]

Duane L. Bliss and Elizabeth Bliss, ca. 1864.

hands were put by its side, then it is wrapped in a woolen blanket and fastened by three straps to the board, one around its ankles, the other bound it across, and the last under its ———. I took a good look at it. I had seen them going by but never could tell what kept them so steady.

The mines, instead of being dug in from the side are worked by means of a shaft being sunk in them. I went down into one called the Imperial mine a distance of 450 feet. We were given one of those two specimens that Duane sent with his collection to Uncle. He put mine in with his but the specimens are all his but two. A man came into the office just after he got the collection packed and offered him $100 for it.

The mine was very dark and close. The miners were working by the light of candles and Duane and Mr. Cory had one to light Katie, a lady who went with me, and myself around. They begin at the bottom of the mine and work up. When they dig out the ore some six feet or more, they put in huge timbers six feet high and work from this [level] until they get another space the same size and then they put in timber the same size as the other on top of them, and this is the way they keep on working, up instead of down. The mountains around here are just like a honeycomb being worked in the same way, but on the outside you can see but one opening from the [hillside] through which the ore is brought to the surface. I saw one place in the Imperial that has been built up in the way I have described—six stories and they were still going up at the time. The timbers are used to keep the mine from falling in after having taken the ore out. I wanted to see how they went to work to make it into silver bars so Mr. Cory, who is husband to the lady who came out under Duane's care and boards here, being superintendent of the mine, took me."

The remainder of the letter has been lost, but this section, which has been preserved by the Bliss family, provides a pleasant picture of the Gold Hill and Virginia City area in 1864.[4]

The type of timbering Elizabeth Bliss describes received worldwide attention. In 1860 disasters were occurring in Comstock mines where miners reached softer earth while following ore veins to greater depths. The Ophir Mine was working at 180 feet where the ore body widened to over 60 feet, making the contemporary methods of preventing the sinking of the roof so impractical and dangerous that work was halted.

One of the Ophir Company directors contacted a young German mining engineer named Philipp Deidesheimer, who came to the Comstock and within a month developed a plan whereby "square set" timbers held up the roof so successfully that engineers from many countries came to study it.[5] The inventor made no attempt to patent it; instead he helped other mines to install it.

The Gold Hill Bank of Paul, Bliss, and Baker was short lived. In

1864 the Bank of California opened for business in San Francisco, with a Virginia City branch established later the same year. The need for a Gold Hill branch became apparent, and in May 1865 the Bank of California also purchased Paul, Bliss, and Baker's small bank.

The Bank of California employed Duane Bliss in various responsibilities, including securing rights-of-way for the building of the Virginia and Truckee Railroad. He became known for his integrity, especially to D. O. Mills, president of the Bank of California, and William Sharon, manager of the bank's branches at Virginia City and Gold Hill.

With the birth of their first child, William Seth Bliss, in Gold Hill in August 1865, Elizabeth and Duane Bliss began raising a family. Also in Gold Hill, Charles Tobey Bliss was born in July 1867, and Hope Danforth Bliss in June 1870. Walter Danforth Bliss came into the world at Glenbrook in June of 1872, and Duane Leroy Bliss, Jr., was born in Carson City in May 1875. WWMEINSR 61873 NEV CITY

Noting the extent of the lumbering operations which supplied the Comstock mines, Duane Bliss reached the conclusion that the forests on the east side of the Sierra would eventually reach a state of depletion requiring logging companies to move into the Tahoe Basin. William S. Bliss's sketch of his father gives this account: "In 1871, he, with H. M. Yerington and D. O. Mills as partners under the name Yerington, Bliss, and Co. (D. O. Mills being the '& Co.') invested in timber land in the Tahoe region and on the east slope of the Sierra along Clear Creek. This association and friendship, like that of the Three Musketeers, lasted until one or another crossed the Great Divide."[6]

In 1872 Bliss moved his family from Gold Hill to Carson City and built a summer home in the small village of Glenbrook. The Carson and Tahoe Lumber and Fluming Company was formed in 1873 with stockholders Duane Leroy Bliss, Henry Marvin Yerington, Darius Ogden Mills, and James A. Rigby, with Duane Bliss as the president and general manager. His long and distinguished career as an important figure in Nevada history started at Glenbrook, Nevada—an interesting settlement whose story had begun twelve years earlier.

Three :
Early
Settler
from
Maine

The little Glenbrook Valley with its mountain meadow and stream, framed by virgin forest and the blue water of its bay, had a beauty perhaps unmatched by any other valley in the Lake Tahoe Basin. The name its first settlers chose was derived from two of the area's principal geographical features—glen, "a small, narrow, secluded valley," and brook, "a small, natural stream of fresh water."

N. E. Murdock, G. W. Warren, and Rufus Walton came to the valley in the spring of 1860, claiming the meadow by squatting on it and building a log cabin. Most accounts indicate that Captain Augustus W. Pray, who had been a ship captain on both the Atlantic and Pacific coasts and who was later honored as Glenbrook's first settler, came there the same year, entering into some type of association with the squatters and purchasing their title two years later.

Murdock, Warren, and Walton were primarily interested in harvesting and selling the wild meadow hay to travelers, while Captain Pray decided to combine farming with a lumber business. In 1861, with Charles R. Barrett and Joseph D. Winters, Pray constructed a water-powered sawmill on the south side of Glenbrook Bay, which, with twelve mill hands, had a capacity of 20,000 board feet of lumber a day.[1]

Captain Pray secured from the government a title to 1,000 acres of the valley, which included both meadow and heavily timbered land. The soil of the meadow section was surprisingly rich—the wild hay crop yielded about one and one-half tons an acre, timothy and clover averaged three to four tons, wheat and barley grew profusely, and oats reached seven feet high during some seasons.[2] Pray also raised vegetables, including an abundance of potatoes, which, along with the grains and wild hay, were eagerly purchased by travelers passing through the valley. With his lumber and farming enterprises, the large, red-haired sea captain was quickly becoming a successful land entrepreneur. In 1861 and 1862 he was elected a member of the Territorial Council of the Legislative Assembly representing Virginia City and vicinity.[3]

The completion of the Lake Bigler (later Lake Tahoe) toll road in 1863 provided a shorter, easier route to the Comstock by way of Spooner Summit and Carson City (rather than the earlier route through Genoa), and where the new road passed through the Glenbrook Valley, its heavier traffic offered new business opportunities. Captain Pray had bought out his two partners in the sawmill. One of them, Joe D. Winters, with Lou L. Colbath of Virginia City, purchased forty-five acres of Pray's land situated about one-half mile from the lake near the head of the Glenbrook meadow. Fronting the new road, they built a two and a half story wayside inn. Christened Glen Brook House, it would be considered the finest hostelry on the lake for the next decade.[4]

In 1864 Winters and Colbath leased Glen Brook House to an experienced hotel manager, A. S. Beatty of San Jose, California. Beatty advertised that the hostelry would be renovated into the finest inn on the Pacific Coast.

An early stereoscopic photograph of Glen Brook House, taken during the brief period when Lake Tahoe was known as Lake Bigler.

In September 1864 Jesus Maria Estudillo wrote in his journal, *A Buggy Ride to Tahoe:*

At 2 o'clock we left the lake House en route for Glenbrook. Our route was along the lake. At 25 minutes of three we passed the line that divides California from Nevada and found ourselves in the territory of Nevada, soon to be a state, I believe. We passed two nice places before reaching Glenbrook, namely Fridays and Zephyr Cove. About five we reached Glenbrook. Here I met my friend from San Jose, A. S. Beaty, who, of course, was very glad to see me, perhaps better my purse. Glenbrook is a beautiful situated place. I prefer it to the Lake House. The situation is on a side of a hill with a nice little brook on one side. The house has a fine view of the lake and is about a quarter of a mile from it. About two or three hundred yards from the house there is a nice valley or flat where some vegetables are raised. The house itself is very handsomely gotten up, furniture and rooms are of the best kind. I was astonished to meet with such good accommodation in this part of the country.[5]

An unusual and puzzling succession of hotel managers followed. In spite of the fact that its rooms were insufficient to meet requests, Beatty gave up his lease after two seasons, and, oddly enough, the

Glenbrook, 1866. (Photo by Carleton E. Watkins)

next two proprietors, Caldwell and Fonda, again operated it for only two years until it was taken over by a Mrs. Mogenberg, who placed bathhouses on the beach and described Glenbrook as "the gathering place for the fashionable of the world."

In 1870, less than three years later, the Glen Brook House was acquired by the Glenbrook Hotel Company, newly organized by William Sharon and Charles Bonner, along with the Bank of California's William Ralston, and managed by Colonel and Mrs. Horace M. Vesey. But continuing the odd pattern of brief ownership, the hotel changed hands again in 1872 when it was leased to Augustus Saxton, who promised that "lovely times now existed, with a dance every night."[6]

The hotel's register, preserved by the Bliss family, contains the signatures of many well-known people of the period, including Nevada's first two U.S. senators, William M. Stewart and James W. Nye; Nevada's first governor, Henry G. Blasdel; Civil War general and eighteenth U.S. president Ulysses S. Grant; Civil War generals Philip H. Sheridan and Irvin McDowell; author Bret Harte; poet

Joaquin Miller; Dan De Quille, *Virginia City Territorial Enterprise* newspaperman and author of *The Big Bonanza;* Miss Lillie Hitchcock (later Mrs. Howard Coit of Coit Tower, San Francisco); Mr. and Mrs. Leland Stanford; and on his wedding night, July 24, 1873, the well-known editor of the *Gold Hills News* Alf Doten.[7]

Alf was staying at McKinney's on the west side of the lake the night before his wedding. He wrote:

My last night at McKinney's and of liberty—

July 24—Clear, warm & very pleasant—One of the finest, calmest and pleasantest days ever seen on the lake—Two boats arrived from Tahoe City about noon with four ladies . . . and several gents, coming to my wedding—The steamer Gov Stanford arrived from Glenbrook about the same time with large party on board for same purpose—Waited about an hour, when all hands got aboard and started out with John McKinney's yacht, the "Transit" towing astern—About 3 or 4 miles out toward the middle of lake, steamer stopped—Boat pulled alongside—took us & wedding party on board, about 20 in all—shoved off from steamers starboard quarter short distance and Rev Mr McGrath married us standing up—Lots of kissing—3 cheers from the people on board steamer—About 100 in all present—Got on board again and went back to McKinney's & landed those from there & then started up the lake—On way back to McK's opened my basket of champagne & used it up—Preacher bottled up a written account of the affair & threw it overboard . . . left for Glenbrook—arrived at 6 1/2 oclock—Plenty of company there at hotel . . .[8]

The legendary stagecoach driver Hank Monk signed the Glenbrook House register for the first time on March 11, 1864. Few, if any, longtime residents of northern Nevada and northern California have not heard the story of Horace Greeley's wild ride to Placerville with Hank at the reins—a ride which became a catalyst for the additional tales about the famed driver for James "Doc" Benton's Carson City–Glenbrook Stage Line. Dan De Quille recorded one story as follows:

Monk, in common with all his tribe, hates the sight of one of those ponderous specimens of architecture in the trunk-line known as the "Saratoga bandbox." On one occasion a lady who was stopping at the Glenbrook

House, Lake Tahoe, had a "Saratoga" of the three-decker style at Carson City, which she wished brought up to the lake. The trunk was about as long and wide as a first-class spring mattress and seven or eight feet high. The lady had managed to get it as far as Carson by rail, but the trouble was to get it up into the mountain. Monk had two or three times promised to bring it up "next trip," but always arrived without it. At last he drove up in front of the hotel one evening, and as usual the lady came out on the veranda to ask if he had brought her trunk.

Like the immortal Washington, Monk cannot tell a lie, and so he said: "No, marm, I haven't brought it, but I think some of it will be up on the next stage."

"Some of it!" cried the lady.

"Yes; maybe half of it, or such a matter."

"Half of it?" shrieked the owner of the Saratoga.

"Yes, marm; half tomorrow and the rest of it next or the day after."

"Why, how in the name of common sense can they bring half of it?"

"Well, when I left they were sawing it in two, and—"

"Sawing it in two! Sawing *my* trunk in two?"

"That was what I said," cooly answered Monk. "Two men had a big crosscut saw and were working down through it—had got down about to the middle, I think."

"Sawing my trunk in two in the middle!" groaned the lady. "Sawing it in two and all my best clothes in it! God help the man that saws *my* trunk! God help him I say!" and in a flood of tears and a towering passion she rushed indoors, threatening the hotel-keeper, the stage-line, the railroad company, the town of Carson, and the State of Nevada with suits for damages. It was in vain that she was assured that there was no truth in the story of the sawing—that she was told that Monk was a great joker—she would not believe but that her trunk had been cut in two until in arrived intact; even then she had first to examine its contents most thoroughly, so strongly had the story of the sawing impressed itself on her mind. Monk's "Saratoga" joke is still remembered and told at Lake Tahoe, but the ladies all say that they can't see that there is "one bit of fun in it."[9]

During the period of unusual hotel operation, Captain Pray was demonstrating his intelligence and mechanical skills. During the fall and winter of 1863, he was busily building the lake's first steam

Captain Pray's home at Glenbrook was built at the same location where rodeos were held many years later.

vessel—laying out the keel, milling the sidings, steaming and bending the ribs, and shaping the other wooden parts of the ship. The steam engine, fire box, and boiler were obtained in San Francisco and hauled to Glenbrook on freight wagons.

By June 1864 the little 42-foot-long side-wheel ferry boat, named *Governor Blasdel,* was operating on the lake, and during the next twelve years she carried thousands of tourists and towed hundreds of log booms around Lake Tahoe before breaking up in a storm when she was washed onto the Glenbrook beach.

During the same year that his ship was launched, Captain Pray remodeled his water-powered sawmill to use more reliable steam power and began building cottages. In 1874, J. A. Rigby and A. Childers built Glenbrook's first store, which was supported on piles over the water—a location which was believed to have had something to do with the mysterious disappearance of Mr. Childers, who vanished one night and was never heard from again. It was surmised that he might accidentally have stepped off the walkway and drowned. Three years later the building burned, and Captain Pray immediately built a two-story structure (30 by 62 feet) in the same place. There was a general store on the bottom floor and a large room for meetings and dances in the second story.[10]

In 1876, Captain Pray decided there was a need for a hotel near the lake and converted his planing mill, which worked in conjunction with his sawmill, into a hostelry which he named the Lake Shore House.[11]

In the small book, *The Wonders of Nevada,* first copyrighted in 1878, William Sutherland, master printer of Nevada, described his impressions of Lake Shore House and the village of Glenbrook in the mid-1870s.

Hank Monk will be your Jehu and will land you safely at the Lake Shore House, Glenbrook, Lake Tahoe. The distance from Carson to the lake is fourteen miles, over a splendid mountain road and amid wild and magnificent scenery. Part of the road lies up Clear Creek Canyon . . . At the Lake Shore House, Glenbrook, where you will arrive at 1:30 P.M. you take dinner and prepare to enjoy the beauties of the lake. At the Lake Shore House, W. A. B. Cobb, proprietor, will be found first-class hotel accommodations; also, a large dancing hall; boats for fishing and excursions; with spirited teams and handsome and comfortable vehicles for the use of those who wish to drive on the splendid mountain roads. In Mr. Cobb will be found a genial, accommodating and attentive host, who is always endeavoring to add to the pleasures and comforts of his guests.

The Lake Exchange Billiard and Bowling Parlors will be found a pleasant place in which to while away an hour or two. W. B. Welton, the proprietor, will be found a very pleasant and accommodating gentleman. The hall is 24 x 90 feet in size. It contains two fine billiard tables and the best bowling alley in the State. A fine stock of cigars is kept and all kinds of tropical fruits, as well as California fruits, in their season. There is an ice-cream parlor for ladies, and a news stand at which are kept all the Virginia City and San Francisco dailies; also, papers and periodicals from all parts of the Union. Row boats for guests are free.[12]

By the mid-1870s Captain Pray had built thirty cottages, a saw-mill, a hotel, a store, a saloon, a livery stable, and a meat market.

The Reverend A. H. Tevis, author of *Beyond the Sierras,* wrote:

Broadside for Benton's Stage Line, ca. 1878.

This chapter would be incomplete did we not refer to the gentleman who has done so much for the business around the lake, and the comfort of tourists who come; we refer to Captain A. W. Pray. He is a native of Maine, where it is said they "plant school-houses and raise men." He was born September 6, 1820. For many years he was master of a vessel upon the

Atlantic coast. He emigrated to California, we believe, in 1853. He followed his sea-faring business for a number of years after coming to the Pacific, and was master of a vessel that ran up the coast as far as Puget Sound.

Some dozen or so years ago the Captain came into possession of vast tracts of timber and arable lands that really hold the key to the lake. He has kept adding piece to piece, till more than four thousand acres of the best land that lies about the lake are in his possession. Nor is his money stingily hoarded. Public institutions of a beneficial sort, charity, churches, worthy enterprises, the needy, are sure to find assistance in Captain Pray. His liberality nearly reaches to a fault. But his liberal spirit is never extended toward an unworthy object. No man more positively repels the idea of giving to or countenancing the worthless and debauched than he. He is a most uncompromising temperance man. Having control of nearly all of the town of Glenbrook, there is not a drop of ardent spirits allowed to be sold. He could receive the highest rents for houses for saloon purposes, but would rather lose money than make it by such means. His standard of temperance is not greater than that of his morals. No man is more circumspect in his dealings and actions before men than he. His summer residence is always open to his friends at Tahoe.[13]

Undoubtedly, Captain Pray's regulations against intoxicating liquor were not popular with some of the populace of the town of Glenbrook. Virginia City's *Territorial Enterprise* reported:

Captain A. W. Pray is the owner of the land on which most of the town of Glenbrook, on the eastern shore of Lake Tahoe, is built. He is a stalwart total abstinence man, and in all his leases stipulates that no intoxicating liquor shall be sold by any of his tenants. The result is that we have at least one prohibition town in Nevada. Many attempts have been made to evade the restrictions imposed by Captain Pray, and to establish free trade in whisky in the little town of Glenbrook, but they have as a rule generally failed. Only the other day there was a battle of some sort, or an incipient riot in the town, growing out of the conflict between thirsty citizens and Captain Pray. Some parties had erected a drinking bar at the end of the wharf, or on a boat moored to the wharf, but the veteran prohibitionist frustrated their speculation by shutting them out with a fence.

A later issue of the *Territorial Enterprise* commented: "A man who is called 'Skippy' was fined $40 in Genoa last Saturday, for selling whisky from a boat near the wharf at Glenbrook. He claims the fine was unconstitutional. They now have a regular whisky war up at Lake Tahoe, with Captain Pray arrayed against old King Alcohol."

Such was the little valley, with its sea captain, to which Duane Bliss brought his Carson and Tahoe Lumber and Fluming Company.

Four :
Carson and Tahoe
Lumber and Fluming
Company

The magnitude of the Carson and Tahoe Lumber and Fluming Company's projected operation required hundreds of men—including supervisors, engineers, loggers, carpenters, mechanics, teamsters, mill hands, and laborers—along with thousands of tons of equipment—including sawmills, wagons and draft animals, railroads, steam tugs, and back-country logging camps—as well as food and shelter for the employees. The final responsibility for all phases of the highly complex organization rested on the shoulders of the president–general manager, Duane Bliss.

Before the Carson and Tahoe Lumber and Fluming Company was formally established, Bliss and H. M. Yerington had developed general plans based on an operation which, in addition to the virgin forest lands they currently owned, would eventually stretch over many thousands of acres on the eastern and southern slopes of the Tahoe Basin. For this vast forest to provide its harvest, three principal divisions—logging, milling, and transportation—had to function efficiently and economically. Contracts were made with a number of operators, including Bliss's friend and former Trinity Center partner, John P. Jones.

Jones had begun a political career by serving in several public offices, including the California state senate, and in 1867 was nominated for lieutenant governor of California on the Republican ticket. His popularity among Republican voters had allowed him to run considerably ahead in the primary, but he was defeated in the general election. The campaign had exhausted his limited funds, and in December of that year, possibly influenced by Duane Bliss's banking success, he headed over the Sierra to the Comstock. Shortly after his arrival on the lode, he was employed by the Kentuck Mining Company, where he proved to be so competent in his work that he was offered the position of superintendent of the adjoining Crown Point Mine in 1868.

Another biographer wrote that Jones was brought to the Comstock through the influence of his wealthy brother-in-law, Alvinza Hayward, an associate of Bank of California executives William Sharon, D. O. Mills, and William Ralston.[1] In either case it seems certain that the two former partners, Bliss and Jones, would renew their friendship as well as have a common interest in supplying timber for the Comstock mines.

During the great fire which started in the Yellow Jacket Mine on April 7, 1869, and spread to the adjoining Crown Point and Kentuck mines, Jones became a hero to the miners and other residents of the Comstock. After almost five days of leading dripping firemen and half-naked miners through smoking and flaming drifts in an attempt to rescue trapped miners, recover the bodies of the dead, and control the fire, on the night of April 12 superintendent Jones found it necessary to block the flow of steam through a pipe below the 700-foot level. A young miner volunteered to accompany him to hold a light while Jones drove a sheet-iron plate through the tube, and the two of them were lowered in the "cage" to the 700-foot station.

It took the two men fifteen minutes to close the pipe, all the while breathing air heavily fouled with harmful gas and lacking enough oxygen to keep their candles burning steadily. "The lights went out as the last stroke fell, and Jones carried his fainting, half-delirious assistant to the main shaft and held him during the ascent. When the hoisting room was reached he dropped his burden and staggered blindly to a bunk."[2] "In rescuing and caring for the miners injured and his kindness to the families of those who perished, he attached himself to the people by ties which can never be sundered."[3]

The Crown Point was in non-ore-bearing rock and unable to pay dividends. From the spring of 1868 until November 1870 Jones hunted unsuccessfully for ore by running drifts on the 900-, 1,000-, and 1,100-foot levels. Late in 1870 the rock in a drift Jones was following began to grow softer, showing streaks of quartz and red, rusty lines. Some 240 feet from the beginning of the drift, the miners broke through a seam of clay to enter soft white quartz containing small pockets of ore. During May 1871, a crosscut from the 1,200-foot level entered the same formation, and the largest and richest bonanza on the Comstock until that time had been found.

The Crown Point stock Jones had acquired made him a multimillionaire; in 1873, the same year Duane Bliss became president of the Carson and Tahoe Lumber and Fluming Company, Jones was elected United States senator from Nevada, a position he held for thirty years.

Among the various species of conifer trees growing in the basin, the most abundant and most important for general purposes were the western yellow (ponderosa) pine and the closely related Jeffrey pine. The sugar pine was valuable for building because of its clear lumber, and the less abundant Douglas-fir was prized for its strength. Incense cedar was used for ground contact

The Glenbrook mills in full operation in the summer of 1876. Captain Pray's original mill is in the foreground.

and shingles because of the resistance of its heartwood to decay, and the abundant white fir was cut for firewood.

Experienced loggers were brought from Canada, to be lodged in newly constructed logging camps, Glenbrook bunk and boarding-houses, or cottages built by Captain Pray. It was not long before two-man crosscut saws were bringing trees crashing to the ground, where trunks were trimmed of limbs before being cut into logs of desired lengths. Wood choppers, many of them Chinese who had worked on the construction of the Sierra Nevada section of the railroad or in mining, were busy cutting white firs and discarded sections of lumber trees into cordwood fuel for the furnaces of Glenbrook sawmills and Comstock ore mills and hoists.

Along the eastern side of the lake, where the mountainsides came close to the shore, logs were dragged by horses, mules, and oxen down to the water or, on steeper slopes, sped to the lake on greased log chutes. Floating logs were gathered and chained into booms for towing to Glenbrook Bay by steam-powered tugs. For this purpose, the iron-hulled steamer *Meteor* was purchased in the East, shipped in sections by rail to Carson City, and hauled over the mountains by

Unknown gentlemen sitting on 12" by 12" timbers by the flume at Spooner Summit. The timbers were milled at Glenbrook and are ready to be floated down the flume to Carson City; from there they will be taken by rail to Virginia City and used to support mine shafts and tunnels on the Comstock.

horses and oxen to be reassembled at Glenbrook. Placed in operation in 1876, and capable of doing twenty knots per hour, she was said to be the fastest inland steamer in the world.[4] Two other smaller ships, the *Emerald Number One* and *Emerald Number Two*, were also used for towing purposes.

At Glenbrook, the company purchased two sawmills and began construction of a third. Until 1875 the lumber was hauled to Spooner Summit in wagons built on the site with wheels made of solid cross sections of logs rimmed with iron. At the summit the

Main flume used to transport lumber from Spooner Summit to Carson City. Note feeder flume providing extra water along the way.

lumber went into a twelve-mile-long V-flume, where flowing water swept it down Clear Creek Canyon and beyond to a lumber yard approximately one mile south of Carson City; a spur from the Virginia & Truckee Railroad provided a means for transportation by rail to the Comstock.

To provide the Carson and Tahoe Lumber and Fluming Company's V-flume with a steady, dependable water supply, a stone and earth dam was built at Marlette Lake (six miles north of Spooner Summit) with a flume to carry water from the lake to holding ponds at the summit. A similar flume coming from the south gathered water from the heads of several small streams.

The ingenious V-flumes, which wound down many canyons on the eastern side of the Sierra Nevada, evoked more public notoriety than most of the lumber industry's other engineering achievements. Some of the interest may have been related to the stories of the wild trips of the adventuresome, who rode planks or crude

Lumber yard at lower terminus of the Carson and Tahoe Lumber and Fluming Company's flume. A spur of the Virginia & Truckee Railroad is in the foreground, Carson City is in the background.

V-bottom boats from the summits of the mountains to the valley floors. Owen McKeon wrote about the Clear Creek flume: "It was possible for an adventurous person to ride the large timbers all the way down, making the 12-mile trip in less than an hour."[5]

The ride which received national attention took place in 1875 on the 15-mile flume of the Pacific Wood, Lumber, and Fluming Company, owned by the Comstock's "Big Bonanza" barons: John Mackay, James Fair, William O'Brien, and James Flood. The skillfully built flume, which began at the company's upper mountain sawmill at an elevation some 3,500 feet above its termination in the Truckee Meadows, was of such interest to Fair and Flood that they decided to have two V-bottom boats constructed to transport them down the steep waterway.

Accordingly, on a mid-September day, Fair, with New York correspondent H. J. Ramsdell and a company carpenter, jumped into the

lead boat as it touched the swiftly flowing water; Flood and a superintendent named Hereford, who had been dared to take the ride,
leaped into the second.

The grade they started down seemed almost perpendicular to
Ramsdell. He wrote:

I tried to grab my hat and hold on as well as possible, which turned out to
not be very well as my bowler went skimming off into the awful void below
us. I now bunched up into a knot with my eyes closed, clenching my fists
until the knuckles showed white, and my prayers came out in a rush of
words. I was waiting intensely for eternity.

Ramsdell was in the rear, where water was coming over the stern
and filling the craft. Suddenly he felt like the bottom of the boat had
dropped out from under him as they shot down a steep grade. On
reaching a more horizontal gradient, he could look ahead to see
"the terrible, but beautiful, vision of the trestle stretching out like a
winding chalk mark, small, narrow and fragile, with all of us suspended in nothingness on this spider web structure."

Seconds later the boat hit an obstruction of some sort, and the carpenter was catapulted into the flume ahead. Fair quickly grabbed
him and pulled him back into the boat. Ten minutes after launching
they came to the worst part of the flume. Ramsdell looked over
quickly and "thought the only possible way to get to the bottom was
to fall and that's just about what we did. . . . One quick glance over
Fair's shoulder convinced me that we were headed for everlasting
oblivion."

The second boat, with a lighter load, had been creeping up until
it finally struck the stern of the leader. Jammed together, the boats
swept across the terminal line at the bottom of the valley near
Huffaker's, ten miles south of Reno, where loggers waited to drag
the bedraggled, water-soaked men from the flooded crafts.

Squirting out a mouthful of water, Fair swore that he had traveled more
than a mile a minute at times. . . . Flood fixed him with a scornful eye and
vowed they had gone at speeds exceeding one hundred miles an hour,
insisting that he wouldn't make the trip again for all the gold and silver in
the Consolidated-Virginia mine. Hereford pounded his ears, shook him-

self like a wet water spaniel, and snorted, "I'm sorry I ever built the damn flume in the first place!"

The carpenter stood, and shook, and said nothing.[6]

Considering the alternative of transportation by wagon over the rough, steep roads, the V-flume was an important engineering development for Sierra Nevada lumber companies. Thirty or forty years ago, weathered sections of the flume and its trestles could still be seen along the old Clear Creek grade, and even today pieces of old planks, a square nail, or a shallow trench still mark the route of the historic structure.

With milled lumber carried speedily by flume and railroad from Spooner Summit to the Comstock, the only inefficient section of the transport system was between Glenbrook and the summit, where draft animals slowly pulled heavy wagons up the mountain grade. Duane Bliss quickly began correcting this situation, obtaining a survey crew to develop a route for a railway. The survey was completed in 1874, and construction was started in April 1875. With a work force of approximately 250 men, the railroad was completed on August 21, 1875.[7]

The rise from lake level to the summit was about 1,000 feet; to maintain an average grade of 2 percent, a 6,000-foot switchback (to gain elevation), eleven trestles, and a 487-foot tunnel near the summit were required to reach the flume station. Owned by the Carson and Tahoe Lumber and Fluming Company, and named simply the Lake Tahoe Railroad, it was 8.75 miles long and was praised by railroad authorities as an engineering achievement. The railroad was operated by three 23-ton locomotives which were shipped to Carson City by rail and hauled over the mountain on wagons drawn by oxen and horses. The completion of this last section of the transportation system allowed an increase in the productiveness of the other divisions of the company's operations.

Bliss and Yerington were aware that one of the Tahoe Basin's heaviest stands of timber lay in Lake Valley, a large area stretching from the south end of the lake up into the southern mountains toward Luther Pass. Matthew Culbertson Gardner (for whom the

Locomotive shops at Glenbrook during the sawmill days. (George D. Stewart photo)

city of Gardnerville, Nevada, was named) had acquired several thousand acres of timberland in the valley,[8] and he negotiated a contract with Bliss in 1873 which called for the delivery of 60 million feet of logs, with 6 million feet due before the winter of 1875 and 12 million feet during each of the following years of the contract's duration.

Gardner built a standard gauge railroad along the west side of Lake Valley which ended at a pier extending over the lake at "Gardner's Camp," which would eventually become the general site of Camp Richardson. From here logs would be chained into booms and towed to the Glenbrook mills. Gardner went into bankruptcy in the mid-1880s; the railroad was abandoned, and the rails and rolling stock were sold.

By this time the Carson and Tahoe Lumber and Fluming Company controlled over ten thousand acres on the south end of the lake and by 1888 it had completed over seven miles of narrow gauge rail leading eventually to what would later be named Bijou. Here, a

The Lake Tahoe Railroad between Glenbrook and Spooner Summit.

strong, 1,880-foot pier was built with railroad tracks allowing logging cars to run out to deep water to discharge their logs, which
were then formed into booms to be towed to Glenbrook.

By the 1880s Glenbrook had grown in population and modern
conveniences. It had one of the first telephone systems in the Far
West, strung partially on trees, which connected it to the Bliss house
in Carson City. In later years the company had only forty to forty-
five customers; it was taken over by California Interstate in 1961.[9]
The town also had a schoolhouse with at least twenty students. In
1882 Frank Stephens Jellerson and his sister Amanda Jane built the
eighteen-room Jellerson Hotel and in 1890 constructed the Dirego
Hotel, which contained the post office, a restaurant, and a saloon.

In the 1890s, the depletion of the Comstock's great bodies of ore
signalled the decline of Lake Tahoe's vast timber industry. In 1898
the Lake Valley railroad was abandoned along with the line from
Glenbrook to the summit.[10] During twenty-eight years of logging
activity, it is estimated that the Carson and Tahoe Lumber and

1870·98

The hillside around Shakespeare Rock shows early-day selective logging, where trees were left in place to provide seed. Today this hillside is heavily timbered.

Fluming Company took more than 750 million board feet of lumber and 500,000 cords of wood from the Tahoe Basin.[11]

Duane Bliss had the foresight to see that someday the beautiful lake and its surroundings would be a great resort area; desiring to prevent its natural grandeur from being spoiled by indiscriminate logging, he issued orders that no tree under fifteen inches across at the base should be cut. In particularly scenic locations, the forest was not touched at all.

One of these undisturbed areas is now known as the D. L. Bliss State Park, consisting of 957 acres with 14,640 feet of shoreline. This recreational area runs from Rubicon Point south around Emerald Bay's Eagle Point. The park includes Tahoe's Balancing Rock, along with giant pine and incense cedar trees, preserved for future generations.

A few writers claim that the Carson and Tahoe Lumber and Fluming Company, along with other logging operators in the basin, almost completely denuded the mountainsides from summit to lakeshore, and they offer photographic evidence. But if one closely studies the photographs of the Carson and Tahoe Lumber and Fluming Company land, looking beyond the apparent devastation, the logged areas are dotted with standing trees under fifteen inches in diameter. Today, a century later, these seed trees look down on their second growth offspring, which have replaced the harvested forest. Although modified by human activity, nature's cycle—the succession of the old by the new—has restored much of the original beauty of the uninhabited regions of the Tahoe Basin.

Five :
A Box of
Letters

From the beginning it had been a close-knit family, the five children receiving love and wise guidance from their parents, and the eldest son, William, showing responsibility for the welfare of his brothers and sister as they passed through childhood and adolescence.

On graduating from the Massachusetts Institute of Technology in 1888 with a degree in civil engineering, twenty-four-year-old William Seth Bliss was assured of his father's confidence when he was made superintendent in charge of the Carson and Tahoe Lumber and Fluming Company's southern Lake Valley logging and transportation operations. During the years 1889–1892 he successfully supervised the large and complex undertaking, receiving the respect and admiration of the men who worked for him.[1]

Early in 1892 a friendship developed between William Bliss and

Back row, left to right: Walter Bliss, Hope Bliss, Miss Mabel Williams (bride-to-be of William S. Bliss), and Duane Bliss, Jr., preparatory to an underground visit to a Comstock mine.

Mabel Williams of Empire, a town several miles east of Carson City. Mabel's father, Evan Williams, came to the Comstock in the early 1860s, eventually becoming superintendent of the Mexican Mill in Empire, president of the Bullion Bank in Carson City, and Ormsby County senator from 1885 to 1891.[2]

Mabel, a very attractive and intelligent young lady, between March 1892 and April 1894 wrote at least 121 letters to William Bliss, whom she called "Will." He saved her letters throughout his life, and after his death, they remained in a box in the attic of the Glenbrook Inn—left by chance to testify to the depth of their love.[3]

One of Mabel's earliest letters was dated March 12, 1892.

My Dear Will—

Yesterday I received a box of delicious candy from San Francisco which I am very sure came from you. It is very good of you to so kindly remember me and I thank you very much. A taste for candy is one of my weak points. . . .

The whist club met at Miss Van DerLeith's last evening. About a week from next Friday I think the club will meet at our house; cannot you arrange your business so that you can be here on that night?

We would like very much to have you.

Mamma joins me in sending best wishes.

Very sincerely your friend,

Mabel E. Williams

A letter dated May 10 indicated a change in the relationship:

Papa was very cheerful last night and this morning. I tell you this because I am afraid you will think he was worried after our conversation last evening. He did not refer to that matter again but this morning wanted to know if I could make bread and told me that I ought to know how to make all such things now. I showed him my ring last night—he admired it very much. . . .

I am quite anxious to know what Duane and Walter will write in answer to your letter. You must let me know. I think they will be as much astonished as anybody. . . .

I am yours lovingly,

Mabel

Mabel received Walter's reaction to their engagement the next day. She wrote Will, "This morning I received such a nice letter from Walter which you must see when you come down. It is very funny."

Travel by Nevadans to San Francisco for both business and shopping reasons was common, and quite frequent in the case of the Bliss and Williams families. A considerable number of Mabel's letters to Will were addressed to or from San Francisco's Palace Hotel.

On May 16 Mabel wrote from San Francisco, in part:

I think I will stay at the Palace all the time I am here as Papa says if he does go to Los Angeles, he will not go for several days, and by that time I will be ready to go home. If he does not go South I will go home with him at the end of the week. I do not want to stay any longer than is necessary and do not care to visit, so if Papa has to remain a week or two I can go home with Mr. and Mrs. Laws who are going home in a few days, or else there will be somebody we know going up, but I will not go alone. About Friday or Saturday I will be at home so will not miss your visit this week.

If you had been on the train [to San Francisco] last night, you would have laughed. Mr. Newlands was on and was very pleasant, talked with me nearly all the way to Reno. Several Carson people came down last night— every berth on the train was taken.

Mr. [Mark] Requa was very nice and arranged things so that I had a whole section, which I appreciate very much.[4] He has invited Papa and me to the theater tomorrow night and we have accepted. I thought you would not object, but I would not have accepted if he had not asked Papa. He spoke very nicely of you to Papa and I am sure he thinks a great deal of you, which he should do.

I have been quite busy since we arrived, running around to the dress-makers and in a few minutes am going out again. . . .

I debated a long time yesterday before deciding to come down here. I had an idea you did not want me to come for some reason or other, but finally concluded it was my imagination and that you did not care. It was four o'clock when I commenced getting ready, so everything then had to be done in a hurry.

I hope I will get a letter from you tomorrow.

With a great deal of love—

I am

Affectionately yours,

Mabel

On May 19 Mabel was still in San Francisco and wrote:

I fully expected to leave for home tonight but there is nobody going up that way we know, so I cannot go. . . .

In your letter you said that if I should remain here four weeks you would come after me. I wish very much that you were here now. But in a very few days I will be home. I have no intention of staying even two weeks.

Mabel finally arrived home on May 23. On May 29 they set their wedding date for September 15. Except for weekends during the next three months, their letters continued almost daily. On September 1 Mabel wrote:

Your letter written before you came down Tuesday reached me today and in it you advise me not to worry. I think you ought to follow that advice and not worry.

Your father told me this morning that you are getting thin worrying for fear everything will not be ready in time. There is no use fretting about it. It makes no difference if everything is not just so. There is plenty of time and what cannot be done now can be done afterwards. . . .

This afternoon I counted the number of invitations addressed. There have been four hundred and twenty-five written and I know of several more that have to be sent.

Mabel's September 8 letter noted: "This morning Mr. Hofer wrote that there was a package at the bank which proved to be the grouse you sent. They look very nice and we will enjoy them for dinner tonight, and thank you very much. I suppose you . . . have been hunting."

Three days before the wedding, Mabel wrote Will:

Two letters from you today, one written today and the one in which you enclosed Mr. Requa's letter with the newspaper clipping. . . .

Ada, Ella, Duane and Walter are here fixing up the room the presents are going to be in. . . . Duane brought the buggy out this afternoon and it is splendid. Have just had it washed and it is as pretty as can be. . . .[5]

I will not write you tomorrow as you will probably leave Wednesday before the mail arrives.

With a great deal of love,
I am
Yours affectionately,

Mabel

The wedding must have been the area's social event of the year. The September 16, 1892, edition of the *Carson City Morning Appeal* newspaper devoted two full-length columns and half of a third to the ceremony and the reception for the two hundred guests.

Last night in the city of Empire, Nevada, in the hospitable home of Ex-Senator Evan Williams, William Seth Bliss and Mabel Evelyn Williams were joined in the bonds of holy wedlock by Rev. Hyslop of St. Peters Episcopal Church of Carson City. . . .

The bridesmaids were Miss Hope Bliss and Miss Ada Tobey, and the maid of honor Miss Enid Williams.

C. T. Bliss, a brother of the groom, occupied the position of best man, and looked almost as happy as the principals. Prof. Krall played Mendelssohn's wedding march, and the sweet strains almost carried the gay party out into the world. Only the immediate friends and relatives of the bride and groom were in attendance at the service.

The bride was dressed in white silk, with a bridal veil trailing from a diamond crescent on her head, and white gloves covered her shapely hands.

The groom was attired in evening dress, and wore on his lapel white sweet peas. The two made an extremely handsome couple.

There is hardly a young lady in Nevada better known to the social world than the Bride, Mabel Evelyn Williams, the eldest daughter of Mr. and Mrs. Evan Williams of Empire.

The young lady is a graduate of Snell's Seminary, and an excellent scholar in German, French and English as well as a musician of considerable merit. Besides these accomplishments she has a natural personal attractiveness that endears her to all her acquaintances. . . .

The Groom, William Seth Bliss, the eldest son of Mr. and Mrs. D. L. Bliss, was [born and] raised in Nevada . . . He is a favorite with every man under him and he is always a gentleman to both prince and pauper, this being one of his most pronounced good qualities. His habits of life are above reproach and the bride in accepting his hand in marriage shows that she has taken great care in selecting a husband whom she will always be proud to acknowledge.

The two hundred guests who attended the reception found that the grounds surrounding the Williams house were lit up from end to end, and between the trees and shrubs hung long strings of Japanese lanterns of fantastic shapes, nodding and beckoning a welcome in the evening breeze to the guests who began to arrive shortly after the ceremony.

Two incandescent lights on each side of the entrance shed a soft light over the merry throng of well wishing friends who filed into the handsomely decorated house to seek the hands of the joyful bride and groom and wished them God's blessing through the life to come.

Everywhere could be heard bursts of laughter intermixed with numerous compliments to the happy William and his newly made wife, who nestled lovingly upon the arm she had accepted as a protector. By nine o'clock every room was full and the changing colors of elegant dresses flashed through the doors and hallways with all the colors of a rainbow. . . .

Upstairs the presents were arranged in a display. . . . they came from East and West, all over the United States, and continued to arrive as long as the guests came in. . . .

A special train was in attendance at the Empire depot to carry the happy couple to Reno where they will make connections with the San Francisco train. After spending the honeymoon at points of interest on the Pacific Coast they will return to Nevada and remain at Lake Tahoe until the season closes. Will prepared an elegant home for his wife and together they will enjoy a life of wedded happiness.

During the following fourteen months there were no letters from Mabel to her husband, later correspondence indicating that she accompanied him on his business trips. In November 1893 she wrote five letters to him in Indio, California, where he was working with Mark Requa on an engineering project, attempting to prove their belief that sufficient underground water existed in the surrounding Coachella Valley to convert the barren terrain to agriculture. Unfortunately funds ran short, and they were forced to abandon their exploration. Later artesian water was discovered, and the rich agricultural area of Coachella Valley was developed.[6] In one of her letters to Indio, Mabel mentioned her pregnancy.

From early February 1894 until April 14 Mabel wrote twenty-eight letters to Golconda, Nevada, where William was involved in a gold mining operation in the Gold Run Creek Basin, twelve miles south of town.[7] In her letter of April 9 Mabel wrote:

Mr. Hofer [Superintendent of the Carson City Mint] telephoned this morning about the first gold received. . . .[8]

Mamma was so excited when she heard about the gold that she wanted to buy the other interests right off and to be sure to ask your opinion of it tonight. She wants me to go in with her, but I told her that is a different matter.

I can assure you, you are receiving lots of praise for the way you are managing—everything.

The time for the birth of their baby was near, and on April 13 Mabel wrote:

My Precious Husband:
Two sweet letters from you this morning.

I knew you would go to Golconda yesterday and told Papa so, but he did not think you would be there. . . .

I am so glad you will be home soon and will expect you Monday, surely. I have made up my mind to wait that long but can wait *no* longer. I am feeling well, but am nervous and am sure I will be all over that when you come, so do come Monday when Papa comes. I will go after you if you don't.

I am glad you have your cabin. You must be much more comfortable. . . . Papa expects to go tomorrow to meet you.

Hoping you are well, and with lots and lots of love and kisses
   I am
     Your loving
                                    Wife

P.S. If you can, let me know just when you will be home. Remember about Monday—

On April 14 Mabel Bliss wrote:

My Own Dear Husband,

Just a line to tell you I am well, as Papa will tell you all there is to tell tomorrow when he sees you.

I will enclose this in your Memorandum book you wanted, as I am afraid you will not get it if I send it by mail, as you will be leaving tomorrow.

Hoping you are well. I am, with lots and lots of love and kisses to my Sweet One.
                      Your Loving
                                    Wife

It was her last letter. On April 17 their son was born. Eleven days later Will's beloved Mabel died.

Six :
Lake Tahoe
Railway and
Transportation
Company

William Bliss named his son Will M. Bliss. There was no middle name— just the initial. Except for the family, few people knew that the "M" stood for Mabel. William's mother, Elizabeth Bliss, took over the care of her grandson.

In 1879 Duane Bliss had constructed a large family home in Carson City, which was later designated a state historical site by the Nevada State Park System. State Historical Marker Number 70 reads:

BLISS MANSION
Built by Duane L. Bliss, Lumber and Railroad Magnate
1879
In its time the most modern and largest home in Nevada. Entirely constructed of clear lumber and square nails. First home in Nevada entirely piped for gas lighting.

[47]

In 1885, using prized sugar pine lumber, Bliss built a spacious family summer home at Glenbrook; and in 1899, to provide a milder winter climate for his family, he commissioned his architect son Walter to construct a San Francisco home at 2898 Broadway—a spectacular location in Pacific Heights with a sweeping view of the bay. The three upper stories provided more than ample living quarters to accommodate all members of the family, who occupied it from the year it was built until 1940.

Late in the 1860s Duane Bliss had already foreseen the day when the usable timber on the eastern slope of the Sierra would be depleted, its yield no longer able to supply the enormous demands of the Comstock mines, and logging would move to the lush forests of the Tahoe Basin. In the 1890s, when the Comstock's ore deposits and the Tahoe Basin's timber resources were both nearing exhaustion, he began planning for the day when thousands of recreation- and pleasure-seeking tourists would come to the great mountain lake.

Resort accommodations for visitors existed, but transportation to the Tahoe Basin was by horse-drawn stages over rough and dusty roads. On arrival at the lake, most travelers depended on steam powered ships, such as the *Tallac,* to sightsee or to reach their destinations.

In 1893 Duane Bliss, at the age of sixty, when most men of substantial means would consider retirement, was ready to begin a new enterprise, an astonishing undertaking in which his family would participate. His plan involved three principal interrelated projects: first, a passenger ship far more luxurious than any other vessel on the lake; next, a railroad which would connect Tahoe City with the Southern Pacific tracks at Truckee, California; and finally a resort hotel which would attract guests from all regions of the United States.

The ship would come first; to build it he formed the Lake Tahoe Transportation Company, with Glenbrook as its principal place of business. In 1895 the steel-hulled ship was being constructed at the Union Iron Works of San Francisco; after completion, it would be disassembled in sections and shipped by railway to Carson City, and then hauled on heavy, horse-drawn wagons over the Clear Creek

Stock certificate for the Lake Tahoe Transportation Company.

Summit and down to Glenbrook. During the year a site for assembling the ship's parts and a marine ways had been prepared along the shoreline at Glenbrook; when the sections arrived late in 1895, riveters and welders immediately went to work. Although winter snows ended the operation until early spring, the ship was ready for launching on June 24, 1896. On June 25 the editor of the *Carson City News* wrote the following story of that exciting event:

GLENBROOK'S GALA DAY.
The Tahoe Launched with Breaking of Wine,
Booming of Cannon
and Great Enthusiasm
Glenbrook, Nev., June 24, 1896

Editor's News:—

"All is finished! and at length
Has come the bridal day
Of beauty and of strength.
Today the vessel shall be launched."

Just as dawn streaked her rosy shafts of day across the matchless waters of Lake Tahoe, Glenbrook was astir. Everywhere arose the intermingled sounds of action, signifying how busily the hands of labor were hastening the final preparations for the ceremony. The steamer Meteor was off for McKinney's to bring a waiting crowd, and conveyances of all kinds, from the dashing four-in-hand to the travelling photographer's outfit, filled with expectant faces, rolled into the little town. Soon the streets were crowded and the joyous holiday spirit pervaded all. Today the magnificent new vessel of the Lake Tahoe Transportation Company is to be launched.

> "There she stands,
> With her foot upon the sands,
> Decked with flags and streamers gay,
> In honor of her marriage day."

In truth she is a magnificent vessel, an ocean grey-hound on a small scale, "with nicest skill and art, perfect and finished in every part." Her length overall is 169 feet, 9 inches; her length on water line, 160 feet; extreme breadth, 17 feet, 10 inches; extreme draught, 6 feet, with a moulded depth of 9 feet, 6 inches. She is supplied with two triple compound engines, of latest design and pronounced by experts the finest machinery ever turned out from skilled workshops. Her displacement is 152 tons and her engine power an indicated horse power of 1500. She has twin propellers, three bladed, which it is confidently asserted will carry her through the water at a speed of 25 miles an hour.[1] No modern ocean steamer is more serviceably and comfortably equipped. She is fitted with a commodious cabin, bar and smoking room, a well appointed dining room, state rooms and toilet accessories, the whole illuminated with incandescent lights, and her pilot house is surmounted with a search light of 4000 candle power.

About 11 o'clock A.M. the Meteor was sighted. It was known she had on board Robert Forsythe, chief engineer of the Union Iron Works, and who conducted the speed trial of the queen battle ship, the Oregon, and Capt. Matthewson and John Bulger, Government Boiler Inspectors, and that the launching only awaited their arrival. The swift Meteor, soon to be supplanted as the fastest steamer on the Lake, showed how swift she could cut the waters, and soon her distinguished guests were ashore. All were eager for the important event. The crowd of sightseers gathered about the goodly vessel with beating hearts. On a dais, prettily festooned and canopied in the red, white and blue, sat Master Will M. Bliss, grandson of D. L. Bliss.

Steamship Tahoe *about to be launched at Glenbrook, June 24, 1896.*

The little two year old chap was to christen the vessel. He held the white ribbon attached to the rosetted bottle of ever sparkling Roederer, which hung from the bow of the ship wreathed in lilac and mock orange blossoms; at his side stood Miss Hope Bliss with the red ribbon, and Miss Ada Tobey, with the blue. From the workmen around and below, under the direction of Superintendent of Construction James Greig, came the sound of hammers. The onlookers stood with bated breath. The hour stands high noon. Lo! she stirs, she moves.

Miss Tobey exclaimed: "I name thee," "Tahoe," shouted the baby boy; "of Glenbrook," added Miss Tobey, and Miss Bliss finished with the words, "and may good fortune attend thee." Crash! the Champagne foamed and gracefully the "Tahoe" slid into the blue waters of the Lake. From the whistles of the steamers "Tallac," "Emerald," "Meteor," and from the locomotives and the various mills and shops on shore there rose shriek upon shriek, the assembled crowd shouted and hurrahed and "Betsy," General Fremont's brass cannon,[2] resurrected for the occasion, boomed and boomed, and boomed!

And so was the "Tahoe" christened. How beautiful she is, riding the waves. "She walks the water like a thing of life. And seems to dare the elements to strife."

It was an unusual day to Nevada to have a vessel launched within her confines. It was a gala day for Glenbrook, one never to be forgotten. May the "Tahoe" bring fortune and fame alike to her owners and builders.

Yours, "REJOICING"

Because the *Tahoe* was operating in interstate waters, Interstate Commerce regulations required that she be equipped as an ocean-going vessel with a chart room in back of the pilot house. Navigational charts were not required to operate on the lake, so the room was used as a private stateroom for the Bliss family and became known as the "owner's room."

Although at first the ship used wood as fuel, she was later converted to burn oil, which increased efficiency and allowed her to run more quietly. Her slender hull was painted white, the exterior of the deck houses was finished with a mahogany varnish, her sloping funnel was cream colored, and her beauty was such, as she slipped through the water, that the piers she visited on her daily trips around the lake were often crowded with admirers.

With the *Tahoe* in service, providing passenger transportation and freight and mail delivery to resorts and settlements around the lake, it was now time to begin the next step of the Duane Bliss plan. From the Carson and Tahoe Lumber and Fluming Company he purchased the tracks, shops, locomotives, lumber cars, and maintenance and repair equipment for the Lake Valley and Glenbrook railroads. All of this (as well as some of the small buildings) was loaded on barges and towed to Tahoe City, the headquarters of the operation. Motive power was provided by the *Meteor* and the *Emerald Number Two*, ships which he had obtained from the lumber company. The vessel *Tallac* was later purchased from H. O. Comstock, who represented the "Lucky" Baldwin interests, and renamed the *Nevada*.

Well-equipped shops for maintenance and repair of both railroad rolling stock and the fleet of three ships (with a marine way on

The Tahoe, *"Queen of the Lake," 1896.*

which the vessels could be hauled out of the water for drydocking to repair propellers, rudders, etc.) were soon built at Tahoe City.

In December 1898 Bliss incorporated a new organization, the Lake Tahoe Railway and Transportation Company, which acquired all of the property of the Lake Tahoe Transportation Company it replaced. All stock was owned by members of the Bliss family, which included Duane and Elizabeth's four sons: William S., age 33; Charles T., age 31; Walter D., age 26; and Duane L., Jr., age 23; and one daughter, Hope D., age 28—all of whom were born in Nevada. Elizabeth's brother, Walter D. Tobey, was also a stockholder. Duane Bliss, Sr., was president and William S. Bliss was named vice-president. Duane L. Bliss, Jr., who had followed in the footsteps of his eldest brother with an engineering degree from the Massachusetts Institute of Technology, was made general manager of the company.

William S. Bliss was chosen to survey a route for a narrow gauge railroad from Truckee, California, up the Truckee River canyon to

Tahoe *and* Nevada *at the Glenbrook pier.*

Tahoe City. His survey for the tracks was so competently done that when, in later years, the rails were changed to standard gauge to accommodate Southern Pacific trains, the same route was followed.[3]

Construction of the railroad tracks and the many bridges required along the twelve miles from the lake to Truckee was started in the spring of 1899 and they were formally opened to traffic in 1900. Several passenger coaches and boxcars had been purchased from the South Pacific Coast Railroad, adding to the company's rolling stock of lumber cars.

Eventually the tracks were extended beyond Tahoe Tavern south along the west side of the lake as far as Ward Creek to haul timber for the Truckee Lumber Company, and a spur for the same purpose was built up Squaw Creek. Although the railroad became best known for its passenger service, the hauling of timber provided a substantial part of its income.

While construction of the railroad was progressing, architect Walter D. Bliss was busily engaged with the final step in his father's plan.

Following graduation from the Massachusetts Institute of Technology, Bliss and his college roommate, William B. Faville, had been given the privilege of additional training by working for the distin-

The four sons of Duane L. and Elizabeth Bliss, left to right: Duane L., Jr., Walter D., Charles T., and William S.

guished New York architectural firm of McKim, Mead, and White. Armed with that excellent experience, in 1898 they opened their own office in San Francisco, where they eventually became highly respected architects, responsible for many well-known Bay Area buildings: the St. Francis Hotel, the Bank of California, the Hotel Oakland, the Children's Hospital, the Geary Theater, the Southern Pacific Building, the Balboa Building, and various buildings at the Panama-Pacific International Exposition.[4]

The Duane Bliss plan called for a luxurious resort hotel, and in 1901 his son Walter gave him that along with a pleasant amount of elegance. The chosen site for the hotel was forty acres of forest land purchased from the Pacific Improvement Company, located one mile south of Tahoe City on elevated benchland bordering the lake. Large virgin pine, fir, and incense-cedar trees partially surrounded the area, providing a feeling of seclusion. Blending the large building—built to accommodate 450 guests—into its forest background, architects Bliss and Faville chose a rustic exterior finish of brown shingles. The steep roof, its large expanse broken by rows of projecting dormers and a singularly shaped tower with lookout and weather vane, was probably the part of the building which first caught the attention of viewers. Wide verandas, bordered by lawns and flower gardens, offered an atmosphere of relaxation in picturesque surroundings. The interior of the hotel—from the nicely appointed guest rooms to the gracious dining room and main lounge with its massive fireplace—was designed for comfort.

The narrow gauge railway was planned so that incoming trains were switched to a spur to deliver arriving Tahoe Tavern guests to the hotel entrance before backing off to the main line tracks, which ran out on the 954-foot Tavern pier. Here the *Tahoe* or the *Nevada* would be waiting for passengers either bound for another of the lake's settlements or else simply planning a scenic tour of the lake.

Over the years the Bliss family's Lake Tahoe Railway and Transportation Company provided an opportunity for thousands of vacationers to reach the lake in comfort. No longer were the uncomfortable horse-drawn stages over difficult roads the only means of reaching Tahoe. In the 1900s, with a railroad linked to steamship service to the various Lake Tahoe resorts, the lake became increasingly popular with tourists and summer visitors.

At Truckee the average city dweller on his or her first trip on the Bliss railroad must have felt a moment of apprehension when leaving the large, familiar Southern Pacific train with its powerful locomotive to walk to the comparatively miniature train with its two or three small coaches, an open air observation car, and a baggage car, all of which would be pulled higher into the mountains by a quaint little engine with a "balloon" smokestack. But when they started up the scenic Truckee River canyon, distrust was replaced by the thrill of adventure.

The conductor, after completing his normal duties, could enjoy being a guide by pointing out places of interest, such as a pillarlike rock where a stage had been held up by bandits in earlier days. During the spring, as the train puffed its way alongside the river and across bridges, he could call attention to the backs of cutthroat trout on their upstream spawning run, instinctively traveling from their Pyramid Lake home more than one hundred miles up the Truckee River to their birthplace.

On the pier at Tahoe City.

The last third of a mile to the Tahoe Tavern sometimes provided a thrill of a different kind when the engine, laboring up the steepest grade to the hotel's higher benchland, was unable to make it and had to back down for another try. Then, with passengers and crew holding their breath and the throttle opened wide, the train would make another run, finally reaching the front of the hostelry. It was not unknown for one or more of the travelers to pause on the way to the hotel entrance to give the faithful little engine a pat of admiration.

Designed to offer a vacation more luxurious than any other resort hotel on the lake, the Tavern stressed comfort and excellent cuisine in a refined and relaxed atmosphere. Outdoor recreation was also emphasized, with fishing, horseback riding, swimming, tennis, boating, and picnicking readily available. Fishing enthusiasts were turned over to experienced Tahoe guides whose reputations were based on the success of their anglers—assuring guests a better than normal chance of catching fish. At the end of the fishing day the catch could be cleaned and packed in an iced container to be shipped to the angler's relatives or friends.

Tahoe Tavern. (Courtesy of James Bell)

The hotel was five years old when a steadily increasing need for additional accommodations required the building of an annex. The following year brought the construction of the casino, with a ballroom where guests and others could dance to the music of popular bands.

National and international recognition for the elegant hotel, the outstanding ship, and the unusual railroad was prompt in coming, and many well-known people added Lake Tahoe to their travel agenda. Henry Ford, about to board the small train at Truckee, showed enough interest in the engine for engineer Frank Titus to invite him to ride part of the way in the cab, allowing him to hold the throttle. Thomas Edison, at the end of his enjoyable ride, "shook hands with the engineer and complimented him on the fine appearance of his locomotive and the efficient manner in which he had brought his train safely over the road."

The dramatic success of the Duane Bliss plan must have seemed amazing to all concerned with it, with the possible exception of its originator. Largely due to the ability of his sons in fulfilling their individual responsibilities, the three steps of his complex enterprise—the ship, the railroad, and the resort hotel—smoothly followed the arrangement he had carefully designed. After his years of providing timber to the Comstock, the accomplishment of an extensive project was not a new experience for Duane Bliss.

Seven :
To Nome

There is a minimum of information on William Bliss's activities between 1894 and 1898. Apparently he disposed of the Gold Run Creek placer mine. Account statements for goods he purchased from two general merchandise stores in Ely, Nevada, dated December 31, 1897, and January 31, 1898, indicate that he was in the eastern part of the state for at least two months.[1]

In 1897 Mark Requa had taken over management of the failing Eureka and Palisade Railway and, as a possibility of saving it, was looking for additional business to which the railhead could be expanded.[2] He may have called upon Bliss, his longtime friend and associate, to take over any surveying or other engineering needs of the project.

In 1898 Bliss returned to his primary responsibilities, surveying the route for the new Lake Tahoe Railway and Transportation Company railroad from Truckee to Tahoe City and participating in the supervision of the construction of the narrow gauge tracks and the bridges required to cross the Truckee River. In 1899, as vice-president of the company, he worked with his youngest brother (Duane, Jr., general manager of the company) on the many details that accompany large-scale, complex projects; and he worked with Walter in developing plans to continue the railroad from Tahoe City to the site where his brother was building the Tahoe Tavern.

News of the gold strike on tributaries of the Snake River near Nome, Alaska, reached U.S. newspapers in the fall of 1898; in the late summer of 1899 word came that the wave-washed sand of Nome's beaches was incredibly rich in placer gold.

With the company's projects progressing under the competent management of his father and brothers, and his five-year-old son living happily with his grandparents, William Bliss, because of his past mining experience, had an urge to see and perhaps to participate in the new strike. With the approval of his family, who may have hoped the adventure might lessen his loneliness for Mabel, he made arrangements for passage on a ship to Nome that would leave as early in 1900 as the breaking up of the winter ice allowed.

The Nome District lies on the southern shore of the Seward Peninsula between the Bering Sea on the south and the Kigluaik Mountains twenty-five miles to the north. The climate is subarctic, with winter temperatures falling as low as minus 50 degrees Fahrenheit and summer temperatures reaching more than 80 degrees. The streams freeze about the last of September and open about the middle of May, while the ocean freezes early in November and opens in the middle of June. With the exception of willows and grasses along the streams the uplands are barren and the coastal plain is tundra, which usually supports a growth of moss and lichens and small brilliant flowers during the summer season. Especially in winter, the lack of trees to break the vast distances makes the region seem desolate to most newcomers.[3]

A party of prospectors discovered traces of gold on the Snake River and Anvil Creek, in the vicinity of what became Nome, in July

1898. One of the men, J. J. Brynteson, returned to Anvil Creek with two companions in September and found rich placer deposits. News of the discovery spread quickly so that by the beginning of the summer of 1899 the tent city of Nome had a population of about three thousand.[4] When John Hummel, an old Idaho prospector, accidentally discovered that the beach sands were rich in gold, about two-thirds of Nome's population went to work on the beach, recovering more than $1 million in the two months before winter set in.[5]

When news of the golden beach reached the states it touched off the same excitement that had fueled the Klondike rush three years earlier. By the end of July 1900, Nome's population had increased to approximately eighteen thousand.

William Bliss's letters to his family written during 1900 have not been found, but from a later letter it seems likely that his ship, which reached Nome on May 23, was one of the first to arrive.

Within the year, mining men with capital began buying and consolidating claims on the Snake River and Anvil Creek areas where, in contrast to the loose sands of the beach, the gold was held in the icy grip of the tundra; only hydraulic mining could release it.

Although Alaska had been purchased from Russia in 1867, by early 1900 Congress still had not established civil laws in the territory that pertained to the private rights of individuals; consequently, during its earliest years Nome received a reputation as the most lawless town in North America. Largely because of this situation, in March 1900 Congress did pass a Civil Code for Alaska; a judge, marshal, prosecuting attorney, and staff of clerks were sent to Nome.[6]

The judge brought along a companion who claimed he was head of an eastern group called the Alaskan Gold Mining Company of New York; between the two of them, they began swindling the owners of many of the best mines, claiming that the ownership of their properties was disputed. Finally mine owners sent lawyers to California, where the Ninth Circuit Court in San Francisco granted an appeal and ordered the return of all claims to their original owners. The judge and his coconspirator were eventually arrested and returned to the states.[7]

Such was the situation in Nome during William Bliss's first year there.

During the cold winter weather, mining operations ceased. It is not known whether Bliss returned to the states during the winter of 1900. The earliest letter found shows that he did return, probably to San Francisco, during the winter of 1901. His letters written aboard the steamship S.S. *Jeannie,* between May 17 and July 1, 1902, reveal the difficulties and hazards of becoming icebound during early-season sea travel to Nome and also indicate the character and leadership of thirty-seven-year-old William Bliss.

S.S. Jeannie, May 17, 1902

Dear Father and Mother:

We have had good luck getting through the ice till this morning but it looks pretty solid ahead. Can see the S.S. Portland in the ice about 8 miles north of us tied to the pack and appears to be surrounded on all sides and will not be able to go ahead till the wind breaks an opening. At present we are tied to the ice but the N.E. wind seems to be opening the ice to the east and we may find an opening over in that direction. Everybody is well and contented. There is a 25 mile wind blowing, temperature plus twenty°, so it is a little chilly outside but have on my corduroy and blue flannel shirt with mucklucks and am very comfortable. Haven't used my overcoat since I started. We are only about 110 miles from Nome but with a white wall of ice between us. We have only seen a few walrus so far. Passed the Belvedere, a whaler, yesterday and Capt. Duvall told us all the whalers were south of the pack and he was sure no boat had got through to Nome as yet. Capt. Mason thinks the Nome City went to the west where the whalers found the ice more solid than here and this N.E. wind will not open it up west of here so we stand a good show to get to Nome City first.

Capt. Mason has a book called the "Report of the Cruise of the U.S. Revenue Cutter Bear and the Overland Expedition for the Relief of the Whalers in the Arctic Ocean." . . . Most of it is written by Capt. Jarvis on his trip of 1500 miles to the northern most point of America in the dead of winter and am sure Father and Babe [William's son] would be especially interested in it. . . . Captain Jarvis and Dr. Call are especially friendly to me since I reached Nome. Met Capt. Jarvis in Indio in 1889. I know several of the whaling Captains mentioned in the book who were frozen in. Senator Stewart [of Nevada] or his secretary will get the book for you as it is printed by the government.—2.00 p.m. Have worked to eastward 15 miles and are now tied to ice with ice everywhere but south, though the ice is thinner here. . . . We must have seen 1,000 walrus this morning. Weather is warmer this afternoon.

May 18th, 4 p.m. Tied to an ice flow where we will stay until it clears up. This morning we ran 10 or 12 miles looking for a lead but everything from N.E. to N.W. appears solid. Still a great many changes take place in a few hours and we may have better luck tomorrow. There are still a great many walrus around us. There are also a number of different kinds of ducks and a few have been shot from the deck.

May 19th. Snowed all last night but the ice seems to be breaking ahead and we are poking along.—4 p.m. We have found 2 or 3 good leads but the fog is thick and we have been "Jacksoned," as the Captain expresses it, several times, that is to get into a blind lead and have to go back. . . .

May 21st. The passengers have a pool at $1.00 per guess as to the time of arrival at Nome. The "Portland" is about 3 miles from us this morning also tied to the ice. A N.E. wind blowing may break up the ice and give us a lead. Plenty of Eider ducks and hair seal around us.—4 P.M. At last we are shut in so we can't move in any direction. The ice gradually closed in on us and we will now have to wait a day or two till it opens again.

May 22nd. Very quiet day, ice on all sides so we can't move. . . .

May 23rd. A fine sunshiny day. Thermometer 72 in sun. Have drifted by St. Lawrence Island; it is 30 miles S.W. of us. We landed at Nome 2 years ago today.

May 25th. It stormed, rained and snowed, all day yesterday. A S.E. wind has packed the ice solid around us. . . .

May 26th. Moved a couple of miles this morning but the fog and ice settled around us again and we are still drifting. In 64°00 Lat. Couldn't get sun for Longitude.

May 27th. Still drifting, were in 64°13N, and 167°38 10 at noon. It is awful monotonous, a little danger would give some excitement but dragging along of time puts one's teeth on edge. We are only 60 miles from Nome and it may be weeks before we get there. The season is short enough without any delays. Today has been a very warm day and have no doubt they are washing the winter dumps at Nome. We can just see the smoke of

Steamship Jeannie *held tightly in ice while en route to Nome in May 1902.*

the Portland about N.N.W. from us 15 miles off. Nome is almost due east of us so we are nearer Nome than they are. One of the boys rigged a dredge with a flat sided can and let it drag on the bottom with a fish line and brought up what looked like tomatoes, red and about the same size, also what looked like some sort of sponge, a star fish and thousands of little red worms. These water are filled with life, top, bottom and through it. It is twenty fathoms or 120 feet deep along here. Wish Babe could be here if every day was like this. There is a low fog over the ice which spoils the Captain's sextant so we got out the transit. There is no trouble keeping it level as there is no motion of the water. The Captain insisted I wasn't within twenty miles because no land instrument, in his opinion, is good for much, but the soundings and everything show I was right, more than that, I know I was right.

May 28th. Haven't moved and may not for a week. The ice is tighter than ever tonight. Passengers are playing shuffle board. The fresh meat is getting a little high but the cooking and provisions are excellent and everybody is good natured. Had a snow storm last night but today is quite warm and foggy. Hope no other boat gets to Nome and out without hearing of us as I know how worried it is apt to make you, but can't run on time in this country.

May 29th. Nothing new today. . . .

May 30th. Stormy cold and foggy. . . .

May 31st. Cleared up but ice still close about us. . . . We are drifting very slowly about 52 miles per day. We are holding a mock trial and having considerable fun over it. Hope Walter has taken Babe to Berkeley. Would like to have gone to the cemetery yesterday. One of the cooks got tired and decided to play sick. The steward called me in as a doctor and I prescribed a big dose of salts and hot tea. He was on deck in short order and doesn't want any more medicine.

June 2nd. The fog lifted about 2 A.M. and the whole coast line from Cape Prince of Wales to Nome, King's Island and Sledge Island were in view. Nome about 50 miles to the east but we couldn't move and are now drifting west with the ice. It is very tantalizing to drift 150 miles, within 25 miles of the nearest land where we could reach Nome, have the fog lift long enough to show us the promised land, then the drift changes and we see the main land getting farther and farther away and the fog shuts down blotting it out entirely.

June 3rd. About 7 miles north of King's Island. . . . Today was as pleasant as could be, 94° in the sun and very little breeze. . . . If we were as close to the mainland as to King's Island believe most of the passengers would try to get ashore but would have to have a boat that they could carry over the ice as the currents around the land would prevent landing without a boat. . . . We have been having the finest sunsets lasting to sunrise (about 3 hours) that I ever saw.

June 5th. I am about to start on a trip to Cape Prince of Wales and I may not make it. If I don't and this letter reaches you, remember that I consider it as dangerous to stay on the Jeannie as to make the trip and we are in hopes to get the natives and skin boats to come to the Jeannie for other passengers.

June 6th. Five of us made the attempt, leaving the boat 2.45 P.M. yesterday and got back here at 5.30 A.M., about 15 hours going all the time and we got within a mile of shore where we found a narrow strip of ice one half mile wide moving along the shore at least 6 miles per hour. It was going so fast the floes were twisting, tumbling over each other and upending, so if we could have reached it we wouldn't have lived in it half a minute but we couldn't reach it. There was 100 feet of mush ice along the side 2 or 3 feet thick but so ground [up] our poles would go through it. We had to turn back disappointed at 9.20 P.M. and Lapp's house and safety only one mile from us. Everybody was abed and don't think they saw us.

Things are looking very desperate on the Jeannie. We are drifting north through the Straits and from there the drift is usually into the Arctic pack and we don't know what is ahead of us. I proposed going ashore to the Captain but he didn't know what to say so decided to go. Called for volunteers and took four of the best boys I could have had. We had a 1 inch by ten inch, ten foot board, pike poles, and life lines. I had charge and took the lead, then came Jim Harrison, Harry Zimmerly, Thomas Campion, and Joe Hern, and we had a rough trip. We were continually getting in to our waists and Harrison went in all over twice and I once. We were working from floe to floe when less than 8 feet [apart]. If we couldn't jump used the board or one would take the life line on a small floe and the others give it a shove for the other side (20 or 30 feet), land there, shove the floe back and tow the others over with the line. In this way we made 12 miles and then had to turn back, and really I didn't think we could make it we were so tired and chilled but more exercise warmed us up and we finally reached the

Jeannie all feeling fairly well but a little stiff. We had more attention and everyone brightened up. Before we had gone an hour we knew it would be impossible to get help to the Jeannie but were in hopes to report her condition. The Captain had the flag upside down (distress signal) and the boats are hung to be dropped if anything happens to the Jeannie.

June 7th. They have been trying for some time to unship the rudder so the ice won't jam it but couldn't get at the key until today and we have it now alongside and feel more comfortable. . . .

June 8th. The mirage showed us the Portland very plain today. Ice the same. The Portland has 160 people on board, crew and all and they must be having an awful time of it. I do so hope you will not get news to worry you before we reach Nome.

June 14th. The Captain called the passengers together on the 9th and explained the situation as near as he could to them and had the government's report of ice and current movements in the Bering Sea and Arctic Ocean read. Said there would be open water where we were after a while but didn't know where the drift would have us a month or more from now. With economy would have three good meals a day for three months but some of the cakes and luxuries might have to be cut out as we were rather short of flour. That he hardly expected to get out before August as it looked as if we would have to wait for the ice to melt. Began getting cargo provisions in shape. I took charge of the fresh meat cargo with three boys to cut [it up]. Threw the spoiled overboard and salted and iced the rest, saving I should think about 800 pounds. Will have to watch it and no doubt some of it will spoil as we have no salt peter. We seem to be drifting by the wind now more than any water current and have not worked north as fast though the wind is south east, but there is better feeling and less anxiety. This morning (14th) the ice got to milling and pinched our propeller, turning it two-thirds over and sprung a shaft so that water came in through a sleeve. It went back into place however and we hope no damage was done. . . .

June 15th. Haven't had the sun at noon to get Latitude but for a short time last evening and this morning and worked by Summer's method, shows we are about 50 miles from Point Hope which would show a north east drift but the lead has shown a north west. The wind is south east, always south east and unless we get a north east wind we will be here another month. To tell the truth I am getting a little tired of it. Hope when reported missing it will be explained in some way so you won't worry about us.

June 16th. The sun has been out all day till 4.20 P.M. when the fog came up. Everybody in better spirits today. . . . We have averaged 15 miles per day of drift, a total of 360 miles and 5° further north.

June 17th. Very disagreeable foggy weather today and southeast wind blowing quite hard. . . . Dick Dawson and I sealed a bottle with a note in it and threw it over, giving our position, 74 people on board, three months provisions, caught in ice off St. L. Island and that we last saw Steamship Portland June 13th Latitude 67° Longitude 167°.

June 18th. Cleared up this afternoon so we could see the land between Point Hope and Cape Lisburne. . . . We are a month ahead of the fleet but I don't think there is much danger. We will [no] doubt drift towards Point Barrow if the arctic pack has left the shore to let us through. Point Barrow is about 300 miles from here.

June 21st. . . . the Captain thinks this wind will open the ice if it will breeze up stronger for 24 hours.

June 25th. Today we are in Latitude 69°5′ Longitude 168°23′ West so you can see we are going north west instead of north east. . . . We are touring the arctic very thoroughly. Everything is noted. . . . The surface water, as well as all pools on the ice, is fresh water. The Portland has been in sight all day and seems to be burning a good deal of coal. We are all worried for fear she may be leaking. We are only ten or twelve miles apart but it is impossible to move because we can't go fast enough to keep the motion from pulling the ice into the propeller. . . .

June 26th. The ice seemed to open a little at 2 A.M. and for the first time in over a month we are able to make headway and worked until evening. . . . We seem to be laying in the lightest ice we have seen and tonight tied to a big white Arctic ice floe with fresh water ponds on the surface. It will average 3 to 6 feet above the water surface so it must be 30 to 50 feet deep and solid blue ice. The Portland only two miles off headed toward us.

June 27th. The Steamship Portland tied to the same floe 2 A.M. Everybody well on board, plenty of provisions but getting short of coal. They saw the Nome City drifting in the ice in the Bering sea but she appeared to get a lead to the south at the Diomedes and get away. We all sincerely hope so. This was June 3rd but the next day they saw a boat north of the Siberian

Coast which they fear may be the Nome in a north west drift. Today the Jeannie and Portland worked ice together but can make very little headway as the ice is very heavy. . . . It is very discouraging but we must get out of this heavy ice. If the wind changes and we are caught between two of these big floes the old boat will go and we will be camping on the berg but we feel safer with the two boats together as one of them might escape the pinch.

June 28th. Still working very heavy ice. We no doubt came into the Arctic with the Bering Sea ice before this heavy ice broke away and it has since broken away between us and Kotsebue Sound. We are working through ice but not much headway in Latitude south.

June 29th. Captain has been in Crows Nest 13 hours. The ice is more open but still large. Have made better headway.

June 30th. Have been making good headway and knew we were safe at noon. Can tell you it is a big relief. Sighted thousands of Walrus which are a sure sign of the edge of the ice. . . .

July 1st. We expect to reach Nome tonight. Are going through Bering Straits at 1 P.M. at about the point we caught the Jeannie June 6th, but there is open water now. We came through 80 miles of ice. We made 40 miles of Latitude but the ice drifted north about 40 miles in the meantime, making 80 miles of ice all told. We are all very thankful to get out, only wish we could let you know before you get to worrying. Will try to send a telegram on the first boat. Everybody is well on boat and I never felt better. We drifted all told between May 21st and June 25th 490 miles, fast in the ice all the time. Will write again from Nome. Love and Kisses to all and hope everybody is well. We are having fine warm weather and it should be a good season for ditch building at Nome. Hope the boys still have the top-kok ditch to work on but they will be short of money as I have it with me.

Your affectionate son,

Will[8]

Eight :
Letters
from
Nome

Although it seems certain that William Bliss kept his family well informed, unfortunately only five of his letters from Nome have been found.[1] All of them indicate that he returned to the states each year during the winter season when Nome temperatures made placer mining impossible. Living in the family home in San Francisco provided Bliss the opportunity to be with his son and to participate with his father and brothers in the planning of the Tahoe projects.

By combining research on general mining methods at Nome with information in the Bliss letters, an understanding of his probable mining operation is possible. On reaching Nome, he would have found that the beach sand had been cleaned of its gold thoroughly enough to discourage any attempt to mine it without the use of heavy modern equipment. Also, it was soon apparent that all desirable land along the Snake River and its tributaries had been claimed.

The coastal plain, which stretched between Nome and the Kigluaik Mountains, was believed to cover several ancient beaches containing gold.[2] But the gravels beneath the thick mat of frozen muck and decayed vegetation could only be reached by hydraulic mining, which required an abundant water supply. Ample water could be obtained from the glacial valleys of the Kigluaik Mountains, but many of the miners doubted that ditches could be built and maintained at anything but a ruinous cost. This belief soon proved to be inaccurate; by 1903 nearly a hundred miles of ditches were in operation on the peninsula.[3]

There was unclaimed land on the tundra plain. William Bliss, using his engineering training and mining experience, probably selected an area for his claim which he believed might cover a section of one of the buried prehistoric beaches. Apparently his judgment proved to be sufficiently accurate; one of his letters mentions that he and a man named Deleray came to town with a "clean-up" of placer gold worth $48,000.

That he did build a ditch is certain. In his first letter to his son (September 2, 1905) he wrote, "We have got 2,400 inches of water in the ditch and working considerable dirt." The letter also mentions a forty-mile round trip horseback ride toward the head of the ditch—a distance which indicates that the source of water was the Kigluaik Mountains.

Bliss also wrote about a "plant." Because of the weather, especially during the winter, some type of shelter was needed to house the powered pumping equipment required to develop water pressure capable of hydraulic mining the frozen tundra and underlying beach gravels down to bedrock and moving the eroded gravels through sluice boxes, where riffles captured the heavier nuggets and mercury combined with the smaller pieces of gold.

For the September 2, 1905, letter to his son, Bliss used paper bearing the heading of one of the three largest mining companies in the Nome district—the Miocene Ditch Company. Oddly, not one of his letters was written on his own stationery.

Nome, Sept. 2, 1905

My Dear Little Boy:

I am expecting letters today or tomorrow via S.S. Victoria which is due. Tell Uncle Walter [Walter D. Bliss] I am sending him some more Eskimo spears. The first one is the kind they hunt Walrus with and these small ones are for birds, seals, and fish. Also sending a net they use for catching seals. It may not amount to much but as it only cost $1.00, thought I would get it and a bow and arrow. He will notice a peculiar cut stick tied to one of the spears. It is a handle they use for throwing that kind of a spear.[4] I came very near getting some Martin skins; think they were worth the money but after the experience with moths don't believe furs pay.

We have got 2,400 inches of water in the ditch and working considerable dirt. Rather think Judge Wood was excited over our output according to Barba's last letter. Expect to do pretty well but doubt it will reach the $400,000 mark, will be pretty well satisfied if it reaches the $300,000. There is 50 feet of bank to move on the Ferrin claim and pay all on bedrock.

Suppose you are having a fine time with your pony. It was pretty nice of the Baldwins[5] to remember you but am at a loss to know what to send them. They can't wear furs on the Islands. Uncle Walter might send them the collection of spears but they don't amount to much.

Day before yesterday I started for the head of the ditch and had to turn back at the Santa Clara Camp, making a forty mile ride. Billie didn't like it very much but came through all right. A forty mile ride over this swampy country is hard on a horse. We had a heavy storm yesterday, started suddenly at 6.00 A.M. and cleared up in half an hour . . . and has turned off cold. Had ice this morning.

This plant looks very pretty at night with the light shining on the streams and the play of colors caused by the spray. They will be through with this bit in a few days now, will then work No. 2 Glacier and should do fairly well with it.

Tell me how you are doing at school, is it easy or hard for you? Suppose the camping trip is over about now and hope to hear all about it in a couple of weeks. Jett, one of our men on the Grand Central Ditch, was coming through the willows the other evening and had a bear raise up in front of him within 15 or 20 ft. It frightened him and his dog left but think the bear was as badly frightened as Jett. He thought it a tremendous bear but very likely his imagination was working. Fink, one of the attorneys, with a party killed 4 bear about 2 weeks ago, the largest weighed 600 pounds.

While in town yesterday I saw the life saving crew put out in the storm and go to the schooner Vega that was dragging its anchor and coming ashore. They seemed to fill the sails before hoisting its anchor. Then up with the anchor and to sea till the storm was over. They got $500 for saving it. Love and kisses to all,

Your loving

Papa

The next letter was written a week later to his sister Hope, whom he called "Betsie," on the stationery of Ira D. Orton, Attorney-at-Law, Nome, Alaska.

Nome, Sept 9th, 1905

Dear Betsie:

I addressed a letter to Neif Pillsbury in your care as I don't know whether she will be on her way to New York or not when it arrives.

Deleray and I came to town this morning with the $48,000 clean-up, one of the bars was the largest we have poured weighing 1,485 oz. and larger than any the bank has made.

The lawsuit fever has broken out again, hearing was set for today but postponed for a week. Don't believe it will bother us much and believe Judge Dubose will make it very warm for some of them on the other side. It is a great town for schemers but I don't think a bargain like ours can or will be broken.

Am anxious to hear about your camping trip, did you see any game or catch any trout? Tell Babe he and I and the pony will have to take a trip if I can manage to stay over a summer but he will have to learn to pack a horse, take as small but complete an outfit as possible and cook bread, beans, flapjacks and coffee as it is doubtful we will have a guide and cook with us. Suppose he would have to have some kind of a gun. Wonder what he would do if he should happen to kill a deer. Believe I was prouder of killing the first mountain quail than most anything. I was going from Hope Valley to the Lake and had to take it out of my pocket every five minutes to look at it.

Hope you kept well and had a fine time.

The last two days have been exciting on account of two or three fires. A boat burned at the wharf as we arrived on the train and a laundry burned last night. I saw two Russian Sable [skins] today that the North Western Co. was asking $75 apiece. They sold 49 skins to Maj. French for $1960 or $40 apiece.

There are 13 Martin skins I am going to buy if I can get them for $100. They are asking $9.00 apiece. They are quite well matched and darker than most of them.

There are quite a number going out on the Victoria. . . . Received the statement concerning RR and Tavern receipts for August. It seems to me the freight receipts are not as high as I would expect. Are they hauling any logs? Hope so and that they can expect returns on that account for some years to come. How do the expenses compare with last year?

Love and kisses to all,

Your affectionate Brother,

Will

Eleven days later Bliss wrote his eleven-year-old son, again on attorney Ira D. Orton's stationery.

Nome, Sept. 20th, 1905

My Dear Little Boy:

There have not been many letters from you of late but Magar[6] has written all the news and I would much rather you took the horseback rides and gave your attention to school than take up the time writing. There was quite a fire a few days ago burning a number of buildings on the main street. A number have already re-built and are in business again. Most of them are saloons and don't think there will be many offices in that section again.

The weather has turned cold, only 16 degrees above last night and considerable ice in the ditch. Ferrin claim is shut down as the ground is frozen and will not wash if put through the sluices. It is cloudy today and warmer, giving us hope for a longer season. The wind has been from the north for the last two weeks almost continuously but is switching around a little today so have hopes for a longer season.

Yesterday Linderberg took me over the rich claims on Little Creek and in some places they are very rich. The Ault is a creek wash and the pay is more uniform throughout the gravel and not as rich as the Portland and Discovery where it is a beach wash and the wave action has concentrated it in a very rich, thin streak on bedrock. On the way back we met J. C. Brown who

[75]

is in litigation with Linderberg over one of the claims. He picked a quarrel and tried to thrash Linderberg but got very much the worst of it. Linderberg finally got hold of him and held him so he couldn't do any damage till they were separated. For once Linderberg was in the right all the way through.

No one has written whether the Indian spears were received. One was sent some time in August and a number of smaller ones Sept 2nd. Would like to look them up before going out if they have not been received. . . . Mr. Leland just telephoned that he had to shut his dredge down last night on account of the cold but expects to get started tomorrow. It has been colder at Solomon than here, the river there is frozen over in places. Am in hopes to get down there in a few days to see the dredge run. Understand it is working fine, handling 4,000 cu. yds. of gravel per day. I have been stopping at Orton's house when in town; his wife went out on the last Victoria and he invited me to sleep and eat at his house. Tell Auntie I haven't heard from her since the camping trip and Uncle Jim hasn't written this summer. It looks as if I couldn't get the bulbs I promised him, the ground being too frozen to dig them in good shape. The camping trip must have been a fine thing for all of them. . . .

Did Auntie and Uncle Jim gain any in weight? I know they had a good time. Love and kisses to all and a lot for my little boy.

Your Loving

Papa

The fourth of the five letters was written to William's father and mother on the stationery of B. T. Dyer, Nome, Alaska.

Nome, July 26th, 1906

Dear Father and Mother:

It is impossible to say when I will get away. There is some talk of my going to Council [Council City] to look up some water rights. Would like to see the country but there is no money in it and I may not go; in which case I may get away on the next Victoria if the lawsuits don't hold me. We have started suits for damages against Jacobson and the Campion Co. Doubt if we can get much out of them but it will set them thinking that they can't rob us with impunity, get off without any trouble, and will hesitate the next time.

I am sending Walter two packages of plants by mail. Believe these make 5 packages all told for Abrahams and hope he receives them all right. Expect to go to Solomon today with Mr. Leland to look at his dredge. It is the only successful dredge up here and there have been dozens of failures. Mr. Matson is here and he can't say whether he will go out early or late and it is the way a number of us feel. . . .

Mr. Ferrin and two or three eastern men were out on the claims with me yesterday.

Am wondering how long you will be at the Lake this year. Would like awfully well to get up there before you leave and it seems to me it would be better to stay quite late as it is cleaner and you will enjoy it more than in San Francisco. Really don't think it necessary for Babe to hurry back to school and would like to know about and arrange for Babe's schooling this winter.

You had better write just the same to Nome until I start out, the boys will re-mail my letters if I get away before they arrive.

There seems to be a number of parties in this country representing capital but the litigation seems to worry them. Still would not be surprised if they invested in some of the big companies. They all seem favorably impressed with the ditch but of course want more ground than we have to work.

Am feeling first rate. Hope you are all well at home. Love and kisses to all.

Your affectionate son

Will

Written on the stationery of his friend attorney W. L. Leland, William's fifth letter went to his now twelve-year-old son with the salutation changed from "My Dear Little Boy" to "My Dear Will."

Nome, July 28th, 1906

My Dear Will:

I received a lot of letters today, the 1st since I arrived as I have been on a trip for the last week or more.

Was happy to hear of Uncle Duane's success as a hotel man and hope the season will continue to improve as it has started and the weather stays good. Would like to be up there with you and enjoying the horseback rides. You, Auntie and I would have pretty good times and I may get home early enough but fear you will be back to school. . . .

Have been around the head of the Sawtooth Range and back on the tundra looking up water power and at some quartz claims. The mosquitoes were awful though they don't poison me to amount to anything. They bothered me at night so camping out wasn't much fun.

The principal business up here is lawsuits and mining and it is hard to tell whether the lawyers or the miners have the best of it. Am writing this in Mr. Leland's office. He is the busiest man in town with his dredges, water power plants, and of course a few lawsuits to attend to. Mr. Metson is busy and we are all anxiously awaiting Court of Appeals decision in the Campion case. It was tried before the Jacobson case which was decided before I left San Francisco, and we were sure everything would be decided before Judge Hawley's resignation took effect.

The water is holding up fairly well and expect to have a fair season. Would like to get away on the next boat but can't say whether I will get away early or stay the whole season.

Tell Auntie I appreciate all the outside letters she enclosed with hers as well as the letters you all wrote. . . .

Kisses to all,

Your loving

Papa

The year 1907 marked the end of the Alaskan adventure. Early in July a well-financed mining company which had acquired nearby properties approached Bliss with a request to purchase both his land and his ditch. The offer was more than fair—the company's representative admitted that the ditch was of vital importance to their project.

For its size, the property had been an excellent producer, but William knew that its richness could end at any time, and he was not a gambler by nature. The seven summers at Nome had provided considerable financial security, but it was the thought of spending future summers with his son and family which finalized his decision.

Nine :
End of
an Era

With the Truckee to Tahoe railroad, the steamship *Tahoe*, and the internationally famous Tahoe Tavern all operating successfully, the average family might have been satisfied with its contribution to the lake; but on March 31, 1906, a new Bliss organization, the Glenbrook Improvement Company, filed for incorporation with the Nevada secretary of state.[1] A Board of Directors—consisting of Walter D. Bliss, president; Duane L. Bliss, Jr., vice-president/general manager; E. J. Pomin, secretary; and J. V. Haley, member—took office on July 6; before the end of the year a start had been made on transforming the remnants of a rough and tumble little lumber town into a refined summer resort.

As before with the Tahoe Tavern, the ability of architect Walter Bliss was an important factor. According to his plan, three of the town's buildings would be remodeled to form the proposed Glenbrook Inn. The two-story, overwater general store, built by Captain Pray in the 1870s, would be moved north of the Lake Shore House to become the main building, housing the lobby, dining room, kitchen, and office on the lower floor, with a dance hall upstairs.

The Lake Shore House, at the south end of the main building, would provide guest rooms—supplemented by the old Jellerson Hotel, which would be moved to the northern end of the main building. The interior of the large Bliss house, no longer used by the family, would be modified to provide still more space, and a number of cottages would be constructed.

Along with the environmental restoration of the little valley's original beauty, the entire project would be a large undertaking. But such ventures were not new or a cause of concern to the Bliss family, and work actually began before the company's bylaws were formally adopted.

A bill of sale for the Lake Shore House, by D. Couillard, proprietor, dated May 1, 1906, read:

I hereby agree to sell to the Glenbrook Improvement Co. represented by Duane L. Bliss Jr. all of my property in and around Glenbrook including all fixtures and furnishings in the Lake Shore House and Saloon, cattle, hogs, chickens, tools and farming equipment with the exception of one buckboard, two horses and light double harness, for the sum of Five hundred and fifty no/100 (Dollars) $550 00/100 to be paid Four hundred and fifty no/100 (Dollars) in check on Mercantile Trust Co, San Francisco and the other One hundred no/100 (Dollars) $100 00/100 to be allowed on hay amounting to that amount which I owe to the Glenbrook Improvement Co.

D. Couillard

(Witness) E. J. Pomin[2]

By the middle of May 1907 the construction of the Glenbrook Inn had progressed to the point where a limited number of guests could be accommodated. The former overwater general store had been moved and remodeled by Walter Bliss into an attractive main building, and the Bliss house and several cottages were ready for occupation.

Glenbrook Meadow with the Glenbrook Inn buildings beyond. (Julian P. Graham photo)

On May 17, 1907, the hotel register of the Glenbrook Inn was signed by the inn's first four guests: Mr. and Mrs. Samuel Center, Alameda, California; Mrs. D. M. Henderson, Alameda, California; Miss M. Byron, Alameda, California; and Mr. F. R. Short, Carson City.[3] The seventy-year history of the Glenbrook Inn had begun.

During the third week of December 1907 William Bliss accompanied his father on a tour of inspection of the family's Lake Tahoe holdings. There were strong ties of respect between the two men, and, at the age of seventy-four, Duane Bliss felt the need to discuss the future of the family's complex operations with his eldest son. In addition to business matters, it would be an opportunity to renew the special friendship that had marked their relationship through the years.

Hoping to accomplish some of the business agenda as the train from San Francisco sped eastward and then began climbing into the Sierra, they discussed current problems and possible solutions. At

Truckee, where they were greeted warmly by engineer Frank Titus
and other employees, they boarded the waiting Lake Tahoe Railway
and Transportation train to find that the company's special coach,
an elegant former South Pacific Coast parlor car, had been reserved
for their use. Files containing summaries of operation costs and
revenues awaited their scrutiny. As the shiny little engine began
puffing up the canyon, Duane and William Bliss turned away from
the beauty of the snow-covered hillsides to concentrate their attention on the records.

The first six years had been profitable, with the income from the
transportation of timber and cordwood to Truckee supplementing
the passenger fares, mail contract, and freight revenue. But, with
the inevitable decrease in available timber, the railway was gradually becoming more dependent on its passenger service; the report
concluded that it probably would be unable to pay dividends beyond the current year (1907).[4] Regardless of income, the train
would continue to be a vital adjunct to the Tahoe Tavern and to the
company's ship transportation business.

Duane, Jr., was eagerly waiting for his father and brother at the
Tavern's entrance. Arrangements had been made for dinner to be
served as soon as the travelers had an opportunity to freshen up.
During the meal, discussion of business matters was postponed
while young Duane provided humorous anecdotes about the hotel's
more active guests. It was still early when the three men retired to
the seclusion of the manager's office, where the year's operation
records and financial reports were ready for examination and discussion.

As in each preceding year, the Tahoe Tavern's success had shown
a substantial increase. The beauty Walter Bliss had created, combined with the comfort and pleasure Duane's management provided, had made the lake's famous resort hotel nearly perfect.

Morning sunlight reflecting from the calm surface of the lake
intensified the beauty of the S.S. *Tahoe* as the father and son shook
hands with Captain Ernest John Pomin and several members of
his crew before crossing the gangplank onto the ship they had
launched eleven years before. They had looked forward to this day
to relax, to talk, to be together. Most of the morning was spent in the

Duane L. Bliss, 1906.

ship's "owner's room," where the father, who still retained the thrill of adventure he had known as a youth, requested details of his son's Nome experiences. Wherever convenient, tourist sightseers had been routed to the S.S. *Nevada,* allowing the *Tahoe*'s crew time to devote much of their attention to the comfort of the owners.

In addition to regular stops to discharge passengers and handle freight, the ship paused at Glenbrook long enough for the Blisses to check the progress of the Glenbrook Improvement Company's restoration. William pointed out that he would have trouble with his brothers if he did not at least make a courtesy call. After pausing an hour at Glenbrook they continued on to the Tavern, where they spent another night, and then took the morning train in order to meet the Southern Pacific at Truckee. There they parted company, with Duane traveling to Carson City to visit H. M. Yerington, his longtime friend. William would take the next westbound train to San Francisco.

When the baggage was being loaded, and Duane was ready to board his car, William felt his father's hand on his shoulder and he put his arm around the older man he loved. The engine's warning whistle blew, and the two men shook hands—for the last time.

The *Carson City Daily Appeal* on Monday, December 23, 1907, under the headline, "OLD RESIDENT ANSWERS SUMMONS," reported:

D. L. Bliss, a former resident of this city where in former years he was engaged in the lumber and flume business, passed away at the Jellerson home at one o'clock this morning after an illness of only a few days. Mr. Bliss had been on a tour of inspection of his holdings at the lake in company with his son Will.

They left the Lake on Friday last, Will Bliss returning to San Francisco and his father coming to this city to confer with Mr. H. M. Yerington, his associate in many of the greatest ventures of his life.

While at Reno Mr. Bliss suffered from a chill which soon passed away; after arriving in this city and while in consultation with Mr. Yerington, he suffered another chill and was immediately taken to the Jellerson home and medical attention summoned. His wife and sons in San Francisco were notified of his illness and left that city Saturday night in company with a trained nurse. Mr. Bliss gradually became weaker and acute pneumonia soon set in and he passed away at one o'clock this morning. . . .

Through his brilliant business ability he has made the resorts of the Lake among the most widely known in the world.

Newspapers in many cities, especially throughout the West, carried news of the death of Duane Bliss. For instance, the *Riverside* (California) *Daily Press* of January 2, 1908, wrote in part:

Much has been said in the newspapers regarding the work and character of Mr. Bliss, but no finer expression of appreciation and regard has been given than that of Judge Goodwin of Salt Lake, himself a pioneer like Mr. Bliss. In the last issue of Goodwin's Weekly he says: "It is sorrowful news from Carson, Nev., that D. L. Bliss is dead. He has been one of the foremost men of Nevada for quite forty years. He and his partner, Mr. Yerington, built the Carson and Colorado railroad; the firm supplied most of the timber for the Comstock. . . . Outside his business he was one of the most thorough men and one of the most perfect gentlemen of the state. He had the full confidence of such men as William Sharon, D. O. Mills, John Mackay and the others who wrought out fortunes and high names in the Silver State. In private life he was one of the most lovable of men. In every position he always rang true. His death will be a profound loss to both Nevada and California, for his business interests were interwoven in both states and his sterling manhood was something to rest on. The blow to his family cannot but be overwhelming, for in his home he was all in all to every member of it. There was no worthier man on the West coast than Duane L. Bliss."

On December 26 the *San Francisco Chronicle* carried a page 2 headline story of the funeral, held on Christmas morning, along with a photograph of Duane Bliss:

The interment was private and only relatives and intimate friends of the family attended the services. Reverend Joseph Wooster officiated. The pallbearers were the four sons of the deceased—W. S. Bliss, C. T. Bliss, W. D. Bliss and D. L. Bliss Jr.

Mr. Bliss was prominent in Masonry, being a Knight Templar, also a member of the Pacific Union Club and the Transportation Club. He was president on the Lake Tahoe Railway and Transportation Company and one of the best-known men in Nevada. Since the early fifties he had been identified with the development of that state, and though of a retiring disposition and averse to talking of himself to his intimates, he sometimes told highly interesting tales of personal experiences and pioneer days in Nevada. His most fervent admirers are the men who have been engaged under him in his various enterprises.

Ten :
Tahoe
Water

At the time of his father's death, William Bliss was forty-two years of age. The tallest of the four sons, he was slim and straight. He had a strong face, his eyes suggesting the self-confidence required to live successfully in one of the earth's more rugged environments. His appearance alone commanded respect, and throughout his adult life, from the logging through the mining days, he had been a leader—even aboard the ice-bound *Jeannie* he had been chosen to head the hazardous expeditions searching for open water.

In business matters, William had been a student of Duane Bliss, and there was little or no change in the conduct of family affairs when, as his father had planned, he became president of the Lake Tahoe Railway and Transportation Company and the Carson and Tahoe Lumber and Fluming Company. Along with his father's responsibilities, he also inherited his problems, including Lake Tahoe's water.

In 1866 A. W. Von Schmidt, a German engineer who had emigrated to California in 1849, announced a plan to supply the city of San Francisco with water from Lake Tahoe. If he sought public attention, he gained it in the arid state of Nevada when he revealed that his project would construct a tunnel through the Sierra large enough to accommodate the Central Pacific Railroad along with two 6-foot conduits carrying 200 million gallons of precious Truckee River water to San Francisco each day.

Over the years similar projects for Tahoe's water were proposed, including a tunnel and conduit through the mountain on the east side of the lake to empty into Carson Valley and a plan for a tunnel and aqueduct through the western mountains which would increase the flow of California's Rubicon River. Such schemes were impractical enough to prevent widespread acceptance. It was not until 1902, under the terms of the new Reclamation Act, that Tahoe's depth and size were threatened.

As its first major project, the United States Reclamation Service organized the Truckee-Carson Irrigation District, which would have the responsibility of transforming Lahontan Valley desert into farmland. A canal was constructed which diverted a large part of Truckee River water from its natural flow to Pyramid Lake and carried it to the Lahontan Valley, where it was combined with the Carson River to supply the needs of the project. Reclamation engineers developed plans for a new outlet channel at Lake Tahoe that would allow the release of water to the Truckee River below the lake's natural rim.

During the lumbering years Duane Bliss had acquired extensive rights to waters flowing into the lake and to the extensive shoreline he controlled. Believing that making it possible to lower the lake below its natural rim would eventually result in irreversible damage, Bliss, with William S. Tevis, who also owned shoreline land, initiated injunction proceedings which were successful in halting the project.

But for those attempting to maintain the natural outlet, the battle had only begun. A syndicate capitalized by a group of New York and English bankers and by the Boston engineering firm of Stone and Webster purchased all of the power plants along the Truckee River under the name of the Truckee General Electric Company. The company also acquired control of property near the Tahoe outlet along with a dam 500 feet from the outlet which the 1870 California legislature had authorized the Donner Lumber and Fluming Company to build.

The Department of the Interior now approached the new owners with an offer to purchase the dam and gates for the Reclamation Service. The power company was willing to sell, but the requirement for a guaranteed flow of 400 cubic feet per second held up any contract.

When negotiations were reopened in 1909, an agreement was reached which included a provision giving the Truckee General Electric Company the right to select a second location for the diversion of water from the lake—widely rumored to be a tunneled conduit that would tap the lake 50 feet below its surface to provide energy for the operation of power plants.

The secretary of agriculture and chief forester Gifford Pinchot strongly opposed several provisions of the agreement, declaring the contract illegal. However, the contract was referred to President William H. Taft without any mention of the official objections, and he approved it.[1]

On the day of the president's decision, Bliss received word of it from a Washington source and immediately contacted Congressman William Kent of California, who secured an interview with President Taft. The president admitted that he had not realized the possibility of a tunnel and had, that day, signed and mailed the document to Stone and Webster's office in Boston. Fortunately, a presidential call to the post office requesting the removal of the letter from the mail resulted in its return—eventually leading to the appointment of a commission to study the problem.

By now the controversy had become of interest to the press, and public reaction to a project which theoretically could lower the depth of the lake 50 feet killed any tunnel proposal.

The director of the Reclamation Service, and the Stone and Webster Corporation, which now controlled Truckee General Electric, then decided to go ahead with a plan to increase the depth of the outlet channel 51 inches—a depth which, along with other serious damage, would affect the entrance to Emerald Bay.

In 1913 the secretary of the Department of Interior met with William Bliss and other Tahoe land owners and California state representatives to attempt a compromise agreement in which the government and the power company would cooperate in building a new dam and gates—with the stipulation that the lake's natural rim would not be lowered.

In 1915 the Department of Interior bought the power company's rights for $129,000, with an agreement that Truckee General Electric would have the right to 500 cubic feet of water per second in winter and 400 cubic feet in summer. The Reclamation Service would have a right to store a surplus by raising the lake level one-tenth of a foot.

The agreement did not solve several important problems, but Stone and Webster built a new dam head and control gates near the outlet, and the turmoil quieted—at least until a group of Nevada farmers, believing they were not getting their share of water, arrived at the outlet with horses, scrapers, and dynamite to dig a new channel. Tahoe residents held the fort until William Bliss obtained an injunction.

In 1924 a meeting in Reno involving the head of the Reclamation Service, the Truckee Meadows Conservation District, and William Bliss, one of the chief owners of water rights, resulted in a contract to permit the Reclamation Service, during drought periods, to pump 300 second-feet of water from the lake for the irrigation season, with the condition that the natural rim of the lake (6,223 feet above sea level) be preserved. Three 36-inch gasoline engine pumps were installed which, between August and October, sent 34,000 acre feet of water down the river. In 1929 and in 1930 the lake was again pumped.[2]

During 1930 the lake level dropped to 6,222.92 feet, which resulted in a confrontation requiring ingenuity.

The story has been told, with some diversity, in several publications. The following version, the one which includes William Bliss's contribution to the affair, started on July 26 when, in the middle of the night, a noise awakened a Tahoe City resident who from his window saw a steam shovel near the outlet rim of the lake. It did not take long to slip coveralls over his nightshirt and start pounding on his neighbors' doors. Before dawn a posse was guarding the outlet, William Bliss had removed the carburetor from the steam shovel's engine,[3] and a messenger was on his way to the county seat at Auburn to obtain an injunction.

The situation seemed well in hand until a contractor, followed by a crew of men, appeared on the shore declaring that he was acting for the U.S. Reclamation Service and was about to blast the rim and dig a new channel. Refusing Bliss's request to wait until the outcome of the injunction was determined, he ordered several of his men to begin drilling the hardpan in shallow water offshore.

The posse was not about to take this lying down. Trouble was about to start when William Bliss delayed any conflict by claiming there was a law which prohibited interference with commerce, fishing, or navigation on the lake. He handed a piece of paper to a fisherman friend standing beside him, who quietly slipped away and, with a companion, headed for the Tahoe Tavern.

After reading the note, the tavern manager quickly searched kitchen iceboxes until he found two large trout. In the meantime, a boat equipped with casting tackle was made ready, and the fisherman and his accomplice, following Bliss's instructions, headed for the outlet.

Within 75 yards of shore, they began casting weighted lures in the general direction of the drilling. The boat's drift gradually brought them closer until the plugs, thrown by experienced casters, began splashing close enough to the workers to make them dodge while loudly protesting. Shore watchers joined in the verbal battle until finally the contractor lost his temper and began frantically yelling that everyone knew damned well that there were no fish in the area.

The two anglers had been eagerly awaiting this, and with each holding a trout by the tail, they triumphantly stood up in the boat— to the shore watchers' cheers.

Eventually, the contractor accepted defeat, and both sides adjourned to the local inn. The two fishermen were proclaimed heroes, the Auburn sheriff arrived with the injunction, and William Bliss bought everybody a drink.

Later in the early 1930s the governors of Nevada and California created the Lake Tahoe Water Conference Committee of six members, three from each state, to adjudicate claims and reconcile conflicting opinions. In 1934, the final year of a long drought in western Nevada,[4] the Reclamation Service prepared to pump the lake by advertising for bids on a pumping contract. Dodge Construction, Inc., of Fallon, Nevada, submitted the lowest bid and was awarded the contract.

Carl F. Dodge, Jr., son and nephew of the owners of the construction company, wrote:

The contract provided for the operation of three very large, electrically driven centrifugal pumps, lifting water into a small coffer dam basin at the mouth of the Truckee River at Tahoe City. Under a fine of $1,000 per day, one pump had to be in operation in nine days, and all three pumps in ten days.

The morning after the award of the contract, the Dodge Company had horses, wagons, barge mounted pile driving equipment and men on the job. Piles were driven to support the platform for the pumps on the outboard side of the coffer dam. The coffer dam was constructed of sand bags seven feet high at the pumps, decreasing to five feet high on the ascending slope at the mouth of the river.

Men worked day and night filling sand bags by hand at a nearby beach area. By day seven teams pulled wagons loaded with sand bags into the shallow water where the bags were placed in an interlocking pattern.

The first pump was started on the ninth day, and all three were operational on the tenth day. The coffer dam basin was filled to a depth of six feet at the pumps and about four feet of water at the mouth of the river. That depth of water created enough head pressure to sustain the desired constant flow of water down the Truckee River for the permitted time during the summer.[5]

Lake frontage owners, concerned about the pumping, appealed to Harold Ickes, secretary of the interior. His representative met with the Conference Committee, officers of the power company, the Truckee-Carson Irrigation District, and the Washoe Conservation

Two of the huge pumps used to provide water for the Truckee River in 1934. (Courtesy of E. G. Schmiedell)

District; in October 1934 a new draft agreement was developed, which included the following terms: (1) construction by the federal government of a reservoir at Boca, near the mouth of the Little Truckee River (a tributary of the Truckee River) to reduce demands of water from Tahoe; (2) establishment of a minimum lake level of 6,223 feet above sea level and a maximum of 6,229.1 feet; (3) reduction of water withdrawals when the lake stood at low levels; (4) specific prohibition of any secondary artificial diversion; and (5) relinquishment by the government of its asserted right to store water above the 6,229.1-foot mark.

Approximately three months after the meeting, William S. Bliss produced a nine-page professional paper entitled "Report—On the Lake Tahoe–Truckee River and Carson Rivers Water Situation."[6] The paper, dated February 1, 1935, contained two pages of detailed measurements as a basis for his conclusions on the past handling of water and his suggestions for future improvements.

In general, with the exceptions of the minimum and maximum lake levels, his findings agreed with the terms of the Ickes committee's draft agreement. The Bliss paper suggested a minimum level of 6,226.35 with an emergency level of 6,225.12. His maximum level would be 6,228.0, which he noted had not been reached in sixteen years. A higher level, he claimed, would flood and damage valuable improvements.

Bliss believed that upstream storage (such as Boca Reservoir) was necessary, pointing out that "no one would be injured and all parties interested would be benefitted . . . if this storage is installed and good business practice and common sense is used in handling the gates."

The Boca Reservoir, on the Little Truckee, was completed in 1939; the Prosser Creek Reservoir in 1962; and the Stampede Reservoir, upstream from Boca, in 1970.[7]

Eleven :
Time of
Change

With a far less sophisticated and formal atmosphere than that of the Tahoe Tavern, the Glenbrook Inn had opened its doors in May 1907. As planned, it appealed to those who preferred a simple yet comfortable vacation environment.

In the prose of the period, an early brochure described the features and attractions of the new Glenbrook Inn:

One of the pleasantest of the unconventional resorts on the lake, every inducement is here offered for those desiring rest and recreation. High up in the mountains among the pines, the days at Glenbrook are warm and balmy, and the nights are always cool. The Inn, with veranda overlooking the lake, contains a dining room, lounging rooms, and a rustic hall for dancing and other entertainment. Many cozy cottages cluster about the

Inn, surrounded on all sides by beautiful flowers, making Glenbrook a place of great natural beauty. Accommodations are provided for one hundred and fifty guests. The table gives good wholesome food, homelike in cooking and service; the ranch and dairy operated in connection with the Glenbrook Inn furnishes an abundance of fresh butter, milk, cream, eggs, poultry, fruit and vegetables. It is the aim of the management to see that guests are so cared for that one enjoys the simple, home-like comfort. Although separated from business cares you are always in touch with the outside world. The steamer brings your mail daily and there is long distance telephone service in the Inn and a daily stage line between Glenbrook and Carson City, fourteen miles distant.

Aside from bathing, hiking the many trails in the nearby meadows and mountains, and riding saddle horses, fishing was a major attraction for Glenbrook guests in the early days. The original brochure gave no quarter: "The fishing at Glenbrook is conceded to be the best on the lake."

Arrival at Glenbrook normally marked the end of an extensive travel adventure. Most guests journeyed overnight by train from the San Francisco Bay area; a small number came from the East Coast. At Truckee the travelers boarded the Lake Tahoe Railway and Transportation Company's unique little train for the exciting twelve-mile trip up the Truckee River canyon to Tahoe City and on to the Tahoe Tavern pier. There the steamship *Tahoe* awaited to provide its Glenbrook passengers with a scenic cruise to their destination. The arrival of the ship—with the greetings to incoming guests, the farewells to those departing, the transfer of mail, produce, and freight, and, undoubtedly, the exchange of as much news and gossip as would fit into the twenty minutes the *Tahoe* remained moored to the pier—was an interesting part of a Glenbrook day.

Perhaps those early years were the golden age of travel to Lake Tahoe.

A 1912 brochure described the "ease" with which one was able to reach Lake Tahoe by automobile: "The usual route from Oakland is to go east on Twelfth Street to Hayward, Livermore, Tracy, Stockton, and then over the Emigrant Gap Route [now

Mrs. Duane L. Bliss and friend in fashions of the day.

Interstate 80] to Truckee. From Truckee the road follows the picturesque Truckee River for fifteen miles to Tahoe Tavern—less than an hour's run."

The road around the north and east sides of the lake would not be completed until the early 1930s, but if one wished to continue on to Glenbrook, a barge service for one automobile and family was available at a rather steep rate of $20 per vehicle.

An entry in the Glenbrook Inn register dated April 22, 1916, suggests what, to the drivers at least, was a heroic accomplishment. "George Sawers, Ray McNamara, Henry Karge, Jack Griffin—9:15 p.m.—in Maxwell Stock Touring car—first machine to reach Lake Tahoe this year. Every foot of the way on own power."

Several years later C. C. Henningson, then manager of the Glenbrook Inn, sent postcards to former guests advising them that "all of the cottages this year have hot and cold running water and a number have private baths. We have also added automobile sheds." The addition of "automobile sheds" indicates that the primitive conditions of roads to the Tahoe Basin were being improved, but for a number of years touring car travel over the existing routes meant varying degrees of adventure and misadventure.

It was the automobile that was destined to bring substantial changes in the holdings of the Lake Tahoe Railway and Transportation Company. Prior to 1920 the constant growth at Tahoe brought increased freight, passenger, and building material revenues sufficient to cover the operating expenses on the narrow gauge railroad from Truckee. Most guests vacationing at Tahoe Tavern continued to arrive by rail, but by the late twenties the improved and extended roads were creating serious competition.

To complete the highway around the lake, the Spooner Summit to Secret Harbor segment, located farther from the lake than any other section of the road, was about to be finished. Engineers had planned for it to run reasonably close to the shoreline, but it would pass over Bliss land. William S. Bliss, believing that too much of the lake's natural shoreline had already been disturbed, vehemently and successfully refused to grant a right-of-way.

The highway was opened in the early 1930s with a ribbon-cutting ceremony attended by state officials. The ribbon was held by six-

year-old Hatherly Bliss and her friend Barbara Bates and was cut by
actress Carole Lombard.[1] The highway, reaching all of the lake's
resorts at a time when most vacation travelers used automobiles,
reduced both the freight and passenger business of the ships.

Mrs. Elizabeth Bliss died April 5, 1921, at the age of
eighty-one, leaving William S. Bliss as the eldest member of the
family. Knowing the respect he had always received from his brothers and sister and their confidence in his ability as president of the
Lake Tahoe Railway and Transportation Company, Bliss gave pri-
ority to the protection of his family's security.

During this period, William S. Bliss's son, Will, began his contribution to the welfare of the company. After his graduation from
Harvard University in 1917, with a degree in architecture, he en-
listed in the U.S. Army Coast Artillery and was serving in France as
a lieutenant at the time of the Armistice. He returned to join his
uncle Walter's highly successful firm of Bliss and Faville, where, as a
young architect, his work required occasional travel to the Tahoe
Tavern to supervise new construction and renovation. In the summer of 1921, while visiting the home of his uncle, Charles Bliss, he
met his cousin Elizabeth's house guest, Miss Hatherly Brittain. It
was a fortunate meeting, for in March 1923 they were united in a
marriage that lasted throughout Will's life and gave them two children, a boy and a girl.

The inability of the Tahoe railroad to haul freight at
a price equal to or less than the trucks with which it was competing
was due largely to its narrow gauge track, which necessitated costly
rehandling of all freight at Truckee—everything had to be trans-
ferred from the Southern Pacific trains to the smaller Tahoe cars.
A complete railroad of standard gauge track was needed as an adjunct of the Tahoe Tavern and the steamer operation, but the exces-
sive expense of rebuilding the narrow gauge could create a debt
which would endanger the company's solvency—a risk William
Bliss would not take. After thorough study of other possibilities, he
devised a plan which, although seriously affecting Bliss holdings on

the western side of the lake, would protect the family's other investments in the area.

With the approval of the stockholders of the Lake Tahoe Railway and Transportation Company, William Bliss approached the Southern Pacific Company with the suggestion that it lease the railroad right-of-way from Truckee to Tahoe City and the Tavern for one dollar a year, with the proviso that it completely rehabilitate the roadbed and convert the tracks to standard gauge so that through service from the Oakland Mole to the Tahoe Tavern would be established. When it was completed, the Bliss family would give title to all transportation facilities to Southern Pacific upon payment in full of one additional dollar.

The Southern Pacific Company accepted the offer, and work commenced in 1926. Company engineers found that the gradients and alignments of the roadbed, made many years before by a young MIT engineering graduate, could not be improved upon. In 1927 that same engineering graduate, William S. Bliss, decided that Southern Pacific had fulfilled the agreement provisions and in an informal ceremony handed the deed to the property to the Southern Pacific attorney—receiving in turn a new silver dollar.

During this period negotiations were completed for the sale of the Tahoe Tavern and other Lake Tahoe Railway and Transportation Company holdings. The Linnard Hotel interests, largely controlled by the Southern Pacific Company, took over management of the Tahoe Tavern properties in combination with San Francisco financiers Bruce Dohrmann, Milton Esberg, John Drum, and Herbert Fleishacker. The Bliss family presence on the western side of the lake was coming to an end.

The sale of the railroad did not include the steamers.[2] The Linnard interests organized a separate firm which operated the ships until 1934, when it was underbid for the U.S. Mail contract by Arthur D. Brodell, who owned the motorboat *Marion B.* The failure to obtain the mail contract along with the increasing loss of passenger and freight business to automotive transportation on improved highways brought an end to the steamers' many years of service.

[99]

Glenbrook Inn, ca. 1935. (Courtesy of James Bell)

In 1935 and for the next five years the steamers *Meteor*, *Nevada*, and *Tahoe* remained tied to their piers with peeling paint and rust spots showing on their sides—waiting to be sold for steel scrap. But by 1940 William S. Bliss, with sentiment for the ships which had served the family so well, had bought the three steamers to provide the dignified burial he believed they deserved.

The *Meteor*, known as the fastest inland steamer in America, was prepared for her final voyage with the hull freshly painted black, the superstructure white. Under orders from Bliss, William Ham of Glenbrook had her towed in a direct line between Tahoe City and Glenbrook. About halfway across the lake the towline was thrown and "the famous vessel sank beneath the waters of Tahoe."[3] In October 1940 the *Nevada* was towed toward Glenbrook's North Point. With seacocks opened and her superstructure ignited and in flames, she sank several miles from the Nevada side of the lake.[4]

The sinking of the ships *Meteor* and *Nevada* had not created noticeable adverse criticism, but when it became known that the beautiful *Tahoe* was destined to share their fate, Tahoe residents expressed both sorrow and indignation. Schoolchildren of the area circulated last-minute petitions, but seventy-five-year-old William S. Bliss had left the lake to live at his home in Piedmont three years before, and it is doubtful that he ever received them.

Again, William Ham had been placed in charge of the sinking. On August 29, 1940, Walter Scott Hobart's former cruiser, piloted by Lloyd Saxon of Richardson's Camp, arrived to take the ship in tow. Bliss had directed Ham to head across the lake for Glenbrook's North Point, the same route he had chosen for the *Nevada* and the *Meteor*. As evening settled over the lake, the *Tahoe* slowly left her pier to begin her last voyage.

Twenty minutes before midnight, Ham boarded the *Tahoe* to open valves and seacocks; half an hour later, at an estimated several miles from Glenbrook, the tow line was removed. At 3:00 A.M. the "Queen of Lake Tahoe" slipped beneath the surface to join the *Meteor* and the *Nevada*. "The *Tahoe* was at rest in the lake which she had crossed and circled thousands of times in nearly half a century of operation."[5]

The vision and enterprise of Duane L. Bliss had brought the Tahoe Basin a railroad that joined the transcontinental line, had constructed the world-renowned Tahoe Tavern resort, and had launched the beautiful steamship *Tahoe*. His four sons—William, Walter, Charles, and Duane, Jr.—had all contributed their energies and talents to this truly family affair, known as the Lake Tahoe Railway and Transportation Company.

The inn, by now, was well established and benefiting from regular clientele. For many, a summer vacation had become a family tradition, with their children later claiming they "grew up" at Glenbrook. The attractions were simple and wholesome, and most often guests stayed for several weeks at a time—occasionally for the full month of July or August.

But the inn, regardless of its popularity, was a seasonal operation and virtually the sole source of the family's income at the lake. The Bliss family still owned thousands of acres on Tahoe's Nevada side, including approximately six miles of lakefront. These properties

Three generations, left to right: Will M., William W., and William S. Bliss, 1936.

had long since been logged, but although the marketable trees had been replaced by a second growth of fir, pine, and incense cedar, there was little interest in summer home development for several reasons, including access. To a lesser extent, large vacant tracts remained in family ownership in the south Tahoe area, again dating back to lumbering days. The phrase "land poor" was applicable in a very real way and would be on several occasions in the years ahead.

Few were spared difficult times in the Depression of the early thirties, and maintaining ownership of such vast holdings of non-productive property had become an almost unbearable burden. While the popularity of the Glenbrook Inn had not diminished, the luxury of a vacation had become impracticable for many families. Capital improvements to the inn were needed but were not possible.

Will Bliss's architectural career with Bliss and Faville was a victim of the period. The slowdown in new construction dictated severe cutbacks in employees, and he went to work for a San Francisco stock brokerage firm.

The second generation of the Bliss family was gradually retreating from active participation in the Tahoe properties. With the sale of the Tavern, Charles had retired to live in Piedmont.[6] Walter was getting close to retirement from architecture. Duane, Jr., died in 1936.[7] And although William was still fighting the lake level and water wars, he had made a memorable pronouncement at a family dinner in 1937. He clearly stated that the changes that had taken place at the lake so disturbed him that he would never set foot in the Tahoe Basin again. He was good to his word.

After a long life marked by early heartbreak, years of adventure in the Far North, excellence in his engineering profession, and wisdom when he succeeded his father as head of the family, the distinguished Nevadan William S. Bliss died in 1941.[8]

Twelve :
A New
Direction

Will M. Bliss was in his mid-thirties when he began to take over the family's responsibilities in the operation of the Glenbrook Inn. Since its opening, the inn's general daily affairs had been handled by professional managers, which allowed Will to continue with his brokerage firm business. During weekends and vacations, he turned his entire attention to solving the inn's problems, including a need for several new cottages and, most importantly, a general refurbishing and updating—for which capital was not available.

There were excellent Bliss lakefront properties in the Glenbrook area which Will believed could be sold without altering the tranquility and unique atmosphere of the little valley. The inn would remain surrounded by several hundred acres of meadow and thousands of acres of forest land. Twenty-five hundred feet of beach front would be retained for the use of inn guests.

In 1935 Max C. Fleischmann bought property in the Glenbrook area and became one of Nevada's highly respected residents, receiving gratitude for his support of the state's university and other institutions before establishing a foundation which contributed approximately $90 million in a wide range of endeavors of benefit to the Nevada community.

Other well-known wealthy men followed to purchase Bliss property for summer homes, and before long sales had made many of the desired improvements to the Glenbrook Inn financially possible, precisely as Will Bliss had envisioned. When sales of property ended, 3,300 acres remained in Bliss family ownership, assuring the protected isolation of guests at the inn.

From North Point (Deadman's Point) north to approximately Sand Harbor and in the Zephyr Cove area to the south, the Carson and Tahoe Lumber and Fluming Company owned approximately 26,000 feet of shoreline along with adjoining back country, which, in some cases, extended to the highest peaks of the mountains to the east. These properties had long since been depleted of marketable timber; road access was primitive, and utilities were virtually nonexistent.

In 1937 "Captain" George Whittell, a slightly eccentric and immensely wealthy San Franciscan, let it be known that he was interested in purchasing as much property on the Nevada shores of Lake Tahoe as might be available. Will Bliss entered into discussions with Whittell's real estate representative, Norman Biltz of Reno. By 1938 George Whittell had purchased over 14,600 acres of lakefront and back country forest land—a purchase that included all Bliss family holdings with the exception of the 3,300 acres encompassing the Glenbrook Inn and a 40-acre parcel in the Secret Harbor area. At twelve dollars a front foot, the price paid was above average at that time.

Day-to-day operation of the inn was handled by manager Fay Shannon. Having eased the Bliss family's financial burdens, Will Bliss began spending more time at Glenbrook overseeing new improvements. His wife Hatherly, daughter Hatherly, and son Bill spent summers at the inn commencing in the mid-1930s. Several new cottages were constructed, the kitchen was completely renovated, and for the first time every accommodation at the Glenbrook Inn boasted its own private bathroom. The operating entity reincorporated in the state of Delaware and thenceforward became known as the Glenbrook Inn and Ranch.

As is common in most summer resorts, obtaining competent employees for the short summer season was an annual problem. Most of those satisfied with no more than a few months of work were somewhat transient by nature. In 1937, while taking a winter vacation at the Deep Well Guest Ranch in Palm Springs, Will Bliss concluded an arrangement that helped the problem significantly and at the same time provided employment stability for those involved. He hired the Deep Well chef, kitchen crew, desk clerks, housekeeper, and wrangler for the summer months when the guest ranch was closed. Food and service at the Inn improved dramatically.

Other key employees also devoted many summers to the inn. Ella Mullins handled the dining room operation, adding such touches as fresh flowers daily on each table. Frank Schneider was to devote forty-seven years of service as year-round caretaker and maintenance man. "Indian Mattie," in her colorful apparel, was capably in charge of the laundry. Hank Emmons, an experienced fishing guide, had charge of the boats. Scottish golf professional Tom Nichols handled the golf course. Allie Imelli operated the dairy and took care of the cattle that grazed through the summer in the Glenbrook meadows.

With these capable employees, along with the Deep Well "connection," the inn entered a new era of popularity.

During the winter of 1937–38, the Glenbrook Inn received a good deal of unsolicited publicity. A snow storm had been exceptionally heavy, closing roads into the Glenbrook area for a record number of days. The two caretakers and their wives were well supplied for such a situation with food stored in a root cellar and milk cows in the barn. But when Frank Schneider, known for his dry sense of humor, met the twice-a-week mail boat and the captain asked if they were all right, Frank jokingly said that they had been forced to kill a horse for meat. He did not think it would be taken seriously, but the captain carried the news to Tahoe City, where it was picked up by the *San Francisco Call Bulletin.*

The report of starving families at Glenbrook made front-page news. The *Call Bulletin* decided to make a crusading rescue mission, and an airplane was chartered to carry food to Glenbrook and drop it in the meadow.

Two days later the well-fed caretakers and their wives heard the motor of a low-flying airplane and rushed outside to see the Glenbrook meadow being bombarded by packages of food. The men grabbed their snowshoes and hurried out to stamp "O.K." in the snow, meaning "We are all right—we do not need food." But the flyers interpreted it to signify "We are all right now that you have brought food." The packages continued to fall.

The report of the rescue made front-page news again. It is not known if the true story was ever revealed.

The operation of many businesses was difficult during the war years of the early 1940s. Qualified employees were hard to find, especially for a nonessential summer resort. Fortunately for the inn, several key employees were too old for military service and were loyal enough not to seek higher paying jobs. Other vacancies were partially filled with pre–draft age college students; on several occasions, Will Bliss picked up hitchhikers on their way out of Carson City to drive them directly to the back of the inn where he put them to work washing dishes. Quite understandably, such hiring practices contributed little to management's peace of mind.

Often guests from the Bay Area pooled their gas ration coupons and arrived in one overcrowded automobile. Rationing often limited menu choices, but most guests overlooked shortcomings, and somehow the inn survived.

In 1946 the inn's longtime manager, Fay Shannon, died; Will Bliss retired from the stock brokerage business to take on the year-round position of owner-manager. Over the years he had gained the respect, even the devotion, of many employees and the friendship of the regular guests. The combination of these ingredients, along with Will's dedication to his work, more than compensated for any lack of formal training in hotel management.

Often those who had spent their childhood summers as guests of the inn were hired as busboys and waitresses when they became of age—allowing them to wait upon their mothers and fathers, who continued to vacation at Glenbrook. Will's daughter Hatherly was a waitress for several summers and later worked at the front desk. His son Bill started as a golf caddy and by 1943 had graduated to garbageman before joining the U.S. Navy.

The inn's pleasant and unique management, along with its comfort and relaxing atmosphere, was supplemented by the outdoor recreation available to its guests.

Thirteen :
Fishing

The discomfort of stagecoach travel to the Tahoe Basin was tolerated by early-day vacationers because of the lake's beauty, climate, swimming beaches—and fish. As early as 1864 A. S. Beatty, manager of the Glenbrook House, emphasized the availability of trout fishing in his newspaper advertising. A later Glenbrook Inn pamphlet boasted, "Trout ranging from one-half to thirty pounds are being taken by rod or trolling from the comfortable fishing boats. We furnish fishing tackle free, but you should bring your own rod. Gasoline launches are always available at moderate rates."[1]

During the years of the early settlers Lake Tahoe teemed with native Lahontan cutthroat trout. Market fishermen operating on the lake took hundreds of tons of trout each year, shipping them to many places where the fish could be delivered without spoiling. It was not until 1916 that the California legislature finally banned commercial fishing in the state's lakes and streams.[2]

The end of commercial fishing and the stocking of hatchery trout apparently was improving the lake's fish population until a mysterious catastrophic fish kill occurred in the 1920s. In 1922 Tahoe residents began noticing dead cutthroat trout floating in the lake and washed up on the shore. In 1928 the shore was lined with windrows of dead trout,[3] and many fishermen believed the cutthroat trout was becoming extinct in Lake Tahoe.

Other nonnative fish, such as rainbow, brown, and mackinaw trout, which over the years had been introduced into the lake, apparently were unaffected by whatever caused the die-off of the cutthroat. During most of the year, the mackinaw live in deep water; fishing for them requires both special tackle and techniques, some of which were developed by longtime fishing guides such as Billy Foote of Elks Point, Molly Moran of Globin's Al Tahoe, Harry James of State Line, and Hank Emmons of Glenbrook.

For many sport anglers, top-lining is Tahoe's most interesting type of fishing. In early years Glenbrook was a headquarters for the sport.

On the east side of the lake, where waves running before the prevailing westerlies had helped to carve out an irregular shoreline of protected bays and rocky points, minnows found food and shelter. And it was there that cruising rainbow and brown trout—the great white sharks of the world of little fishes—found their best hunting.

Top-line tackle is not as specialized as deep-line equipment. Trolling rods of various lengths and weights are used; after its invention, the spinning rod and reel probably became the most popular. Reels large enough to hold at least one hundred yards of five- to ten-pound test monofilament line are desirable, allowing the lure to trail a considerable distance behind the boat while providing enough backup line to supply slack to a snag or to fight a large fish.

Individuals have their own opinions of the best artificial lures for Tahoe, with most of their choices based on prior successes. Many

Fishing at Glenbrook Point.

imitation fish, crayfish, and other creatures are for sale, some of which never existed in Tahoe or any other lake in the world, but one old-timer claims that one of the oldest lures—a small spoon (spinner) trailing a snelled baited hook—will catch as many fish as any of the new creations.

Experienced anglers prefer early morning and evening fishing when the lake is most apt to be calm and the trout more actively feeding. Most trolling is done in water shallow enough for the bottom of the lake to be seen. In a rocky area not far from Glenbrook Bay it is sometimes possible to watch a school of chubs being herded like a flock of sheep by several large rainbow trout.

William T. "Bill" Daniel of Reno, an experienced angler in both deep-lining and top-lining for Tahoe trout, tells of the day in 1931 when he was taking a friend for a boat ride and saw an unusually large trout loafing along the bottom of a bay. Bill had not intended to fish; his tackle had been left in his car, which was about fifteen minutes away. But it was the largest fish he had seen that year, and he headed for his tackle.

He must have set some kind of a record. Thirty-five minutes later he was fishing and five minutes after that he was fighting an eight-pound cutthroat trout.

Bill also remembers the day he and two companions top-lined north of Glenbrook:

We started out early; the lake's surface was calm. I had two long-time friends with me; all of us were college students.

From the Glenbrook pier we trolled across the bay and around North Point which since early days has been known as Dead Man's Point. Lake currents controlled by prevailing winds bring flotsam there from boat accidents occurring further south.

The fishing was quite good that morning; during the next few hours we landed several nice fish. I mentally can still see those rainbow, with their silvery, steelhead coloring,[4] shooting out of the water, often shaking the hook loose.

About noon, we went ashore at a beautiful little bay, known as Skunk Harbor, where we planned to have lunch and to relax—until we noticed that the gentle breeze we had been enjoying was getting stronger.

By the time we got back to the boat and shoved off, we could see whitecaps beyond the bay, and before we reached North Point we were in heavy waves. We should have turned back, but we kept going until we were off the point where, suddenly, the waves were too large and the troughs too deep. Our motor was not powerful enough to keep us away from the rocks, and we had gone beyond a place of no return.

One of us saw a small opening between the rocks with a short strip of sand beyond, and we turned toward it. I don't know how we managed to do it, but we went through that narrow space without scraping the boat—a wave took us part way up on the beach. The boat had shipped some water, but we were able to drag it above the wave line and tip it over to drain it.

I knew the wind would not decrease before evening, and also knew that by then Glenbrook guide Hank Emmons would be out looking for us. My two companions had a dinner engagement, so I suggested that they hike over the point and on to Glenbrook to reassure everyone we were safe. I would stay with the boat to see if the wind died down, and, if it was still blowing at dusk, would leave the boat and head for Glenbrook.

We had gotten up early that morning, and sitting on the beach watching

Longtime Tahoe fisherman William T. Daniel with deep-line tackle.

the waves put me to sleep. I didn't awaken until shortly after seven o'clock, and I guess I was sort of bleary eyed when I looked out at the lake and decided the waves had subsided to where I could use the boat. I pushed it down to the water, started the motor, got out through the rocks, and found that the lake was still rough—the waves twice as large as they had looked from shore.

To give the boat more stability, I stretched out flat along the bottom in a position where I could reach the motor and see ahead to steer. I barely cleared the point's rocks but got out on the bay and made it across without taking water. Hank was waiting for me at the pier.

So the day, regardless of carelessness, turned out all right. A lake is an enjoyable part of the natural world, but sometimes water and wind are a dangerous mixture.

Fourteen :
Rodeos

In the late 1930s Allie Imelli was summer pasturing some 300 head of cattle in the surrounding meadows—China Garden, Upper Pray, Lower Pray, and the large Glenbrook meadow in the center of which stood the Glenbrook Inn, the cottages, and numerous maintenance buildings. Allie's dairy herd supplied the inn with milk and cream on a daily basis.

Johnny Vance, who had charge of the riding stable, was a Rodeo Cowboy Association caliber roper, having competed in many major rodeos. Allie Imelli was a good working roper, and Will Bliss was a somewhat frustrated, though relentless, weekend roper. He conceived the idea of constructing a roping arena close to the hay barn and apple orchard for practice and for the entertainment of the inn's guests.

During evenings in 1939 they and other employees—using scrap

Hatherly and Will Bliss on deck of stable tack room where ropers lined up to pay entry fees on rodeo day. (Julian P. Graham photo)

lumber and young pine trees for fencing and cut and split cedar for posts, created an arena which satisfactorily filled their needs. Cattle chutes and catch pens were added, and before long Allie's cows and calves could no longer count on endless days of peaceful grazing.

Many of the guests had never seen calf roping and team roping before and "practice" became a popular attraction. Cowboy friends of Will Bliss from nearby ranches in Carson, Smith, and Mason valleys began to show up on weekends, and the Glenbrook rodeos were born. Although they were simple family get-togethers, they always remained competitive.

The setting, next to the apple orchard in the large meadow at the base of the surrounding mountains and Shakespeare Rock, was spectacular. A three-row bleacher stand was constructed, and an announcer's stand was built above the calf chutes. Entry fees were collected in the stable tack room by Will Bliss, his wife Hatherly, and other members of the family. The fee money was divided into prizes

Chris Cordes calf-roping at Glenbrook rodeo.

to be returned to the ropers for first, second, third, and sometimes fourth place in the competition.

As many as eighty to a hundred competitors began taking part in the event; the apple orchard was jammed with horse trailers. To the accompaniment of a scratchy, 78-RPM recording of "The Star-Spangled Banner," those cowboys and guests who wished to take part made a very informal Grand Entry. Will's daughter Hatherly led with the Stars and Stripes; often her best friend of the moment rode with her, carrying a large green flag displaying a white letter "G."

A loudspeaker was acquired, and Will Bliss and his friends (Graham Hollister, Frazer West, and others) timed the events and kept

Will Bliss, camp cook for Glenbrook breakfast rides.

up a spur-of-the-moment commentary. Preparatory to roping, cattle were prodded from catch pens into the chutes by the cowboys and by volunteer children, often many more than were needed. Flagging in the arena was also by volunteers, adding a special interest to a unique and popular roping show.

Within a few years three Sunday rodeos were held at Glenbrook each summer, with calf and team roping, steer stopping, a girls' barrel race, and occasionally wild cow milking. Entry fees were always divided and returned to the cowboys, no admission was ever charged spectators, and the presence of a sheriff's deputy was never considered.

As the rodeos at Glenbrook grew in popularity among the guests, interest in horseback riding increased. In 1942 Johnny Vance hired Jack Morgan to assist him in handling the larger number of riders.

Jack was Wyoming born, a leathery, wiry individual—the quintessential cowboy blessed with native wisdom, warmth, intelligence, and sense of humor. He had little formal education but had learned well from his many years on cattle and dude ranches in Montana, Wyoming, and California. Jack's tales were told with an imaginative vocabulary and a sentence structure that was always somewhat questionable. His first impression of Glenbrook was: "It sure beats making a dry camp out of a wet saddle blanket." He was destined to become one of Glenbrook's most colorful, loyal, and memorable employees over the balance of his life, some thirty-five years.

All-day picnic rides to Genoa Peak to the south and Blisster Beach to the north were booked well in advance, but perhaps the most popular events were breakfast rides. Twenty-five or so guests received an early call and watched the day break while riding through China Gardens, Devil's Gate, and eventually Upper Pray Meadow.

A hitch rack nailed to pine trees, picnic tables, camp stools, and a charcoal fire with a grill in an open pit awaited them. Often Will Bliss was camp cook. He was seldom happier than when taking part in an outdoor activity.[1]

Fifteen :
Golf and
Tennis

An article by Nick Seitz in the May 1990 issue of *Golf Digest* magazine noted:

The finest nine-hole courses are a joy. Royal Worlington 50 miles outside London may well be Number 1. Other beauties include Whitinsville in western Massachusetts, a pristine Donald Ross masterpiece—Sea Ranch on the northern California Highlands—Hillcrest in Batesville, Indiana—Glenbrook on the eastern shore of Lake Tahoe, Nevada, about which Ben Hogan once enthused.

Perched high on the hillside, the Glenbrook golf course ninth tee, with its fairway far below bending among giant pine trees to a green near the lake, offered a picturesque view. But the scenery went unnoticed by those who watched the great Ben Hogan select a club one summer day in 1948.

18 Hole

Exhibition

Golf Match

at

GLENBROOK

Lake Tahoe   Nevada

Featuring

BEN HOGAN

WESTERN OPEN CHAMPION
U. S. OPEN CHAMPION
P. G. A. CHAMPION

TUESDAY, SEPT. 7, 1:30 P.M.

Admission $1.50
Federal Tax   .30
            $1.80

RECORD-COURIER ◆ GARDNERVILLE NEVADA

Broadside for exhibition golf match at Glenbrook, 1948.

During the preceding week, while playing in a tournament at the Washoe County Golf Course in Reno, Hogan had been persuaded to stop for a clinic and an eighteen-hole exhibition round at Glenbrook on his way back to Texas. For a small fee to cover additional expenses, he gave his enthusiastic spectators an especially pleasant day—scoring five under par on the eighteen holes and providing a clinic with demonstration shots for several additional hours. After having dinner with the Bliss family and staying overnight at the inn, he and his wife were on their way back to Texas early the next morning.

Construction on the Glenbrook golf course started in 1925, twenty-three years before the great golfer played there. The course was probably designed to use much of the available natural meadow land, but many trees had to be felled—their stumps uprooted with the help of a Fordson tractor and piled in the center of future fairways to be burned during the following winter. What had been the ice pond for the Inn was drained, and during 1926 fairways were graded and tees and greens were built. The course was seeded before the end of the growing season, and play began in 1927.

Over the years the course was managed by a number of capable professionals including Louis Bertoloni, Tom Nichols (of St. Andrews, Scotland), Floyd Hudson, and Joe Moniz. It was a unique and interesting nine-hole course which, with two tee areas for each hole, gave players an eighteen-hole game. Most of the fairways were shorter than average, but heavily forested roughs brought high scores to those who did not hit a straight ball. There were temptations to take short cuts to the greens by flying the ball over the tops of tall pines, which many golfers—to their sorrow—could not resist. And there was a small fir on the right side of the fourth fairway whose upright needles were uncannily able to hold onto a ball which a sliced shot put there. After play ended on a busy day, some of the caddies, including young Bill Bliss, would climb the tree to shake its branches and fill their pockets with the balls which rained down. Today that tree is taller but is still fielding golf balls.

It was a special course which could be walked and played in about four hours—allowing time for swimming and other activities. The

Caddy house at the Glenbrook golf course. (Julian P. Graham photo)

beauty of the environment and the cool breeze coming in from the
lake added to the enjoyment of playing golf at Glenbrook.

Former caddies can tell good stories. Distinguished Nevada author Robert Laxalt was a Glenbrook caddy in the late 1930s, and he
recalls those pleasant days:

Being a caddy at Glenbrook was hard work but enjoyable. Other Carson City kids also earned their spending money by caddying there. We were picked up by the caddy master each morning and taken up to the course before play began. We would work all day if there were enough golfers, and the inn would provide us with a lunch, which was ample for growing kids with large appetites.

Most of our golfers were polite and quiet people who, even at our young age, impressed us. Now and then a well-known person or even a celebrity would play the course, and that would be especially interesting. Max Baer, the former heavyweight boxing champion of the world, was our favorite.

Max would come to visit with us. I remember that one day he told us how fortunate we were to have to work—to be thankful we weren't born rich. He said, "Those are the guys who throw themselves out of windows of tall buildings when the going gets rough. You guys know how to work, so nothing like that is going to scare you that bad." The memory of what occurred after the stock market crash was on his mind.

Max was a little larger than a giant—a tall man with a statuesque body, broad shoulders, long arms, thin waist, prizefighter's broken nose, curly (almost kinky) hair, and always a big smile on his face. He told us many things, but one day he told us something that any sportswriter in the world would have given his month's salary to hear.

Before Max came to visit us that day we had been talking about a rumor someone had heard that Max had intentionally taken the ten count on one knee when he lost the championship fight to Joe Louis. We were certain he would not lie down, but being kids, we were pretty frank and not very diplomatic, and, feeling certain the answer would be no, one of us asked, "Max, did you lie down in the fight with Joe Louis?"

Max looked directly at us and didn't hesitate with his answer, "Damn right I did. After the first four times he hit me I decided I wanted my family to recognize me the next day, so I took the count."

It was a remarkable revelation to us—we just stared at him; we couldn't accept the possibility of our hero lying down to anyone in the world. But then as we looked at the fight scars around his mouth and eyes, and that broken nose, we began to realize that there had been a possibility of his family not recognizing him the next day.

Another factor that made it easier for us to understand was our respect for Joe Louis. We considered him a perfect fighter, poetry in motion with that lightning fast jab. He was an honorable man, a good man, a credit to boxing.

I remember Max playing the course. He would practice a few swings with irons on the side of the first tee, and the size of the divot would astonish us. He hit a ball about as long as any professional at that time—about three hundred yards.

There were other people who were our favorites, such as Major Max C. Fleischmann, who was not a heavy tipper, but we accepted him—no one resented his tipping. We knew he was immensely wealthy, but he would tip a dime. I think he once tipped a quarter and another time a candy bar.

Major Fleischmann was a little embarrassed about his golf game, but I wouldn't have been. He was not a long hitter, but he hit the ball straight and caddying for him did not entail searching through the woods for it. When he came to the final hole he was not far over par—always a very respectable score. He was kind to us kids; he was a kind man.

A. K. Bourne, head of the Singer Sewing Machine Company, was a bulky man who was also kind to us caddies. He was a good tipper and a very strong golfer.

There were no carts in those days, so a caddy had to carry one or two bags, some days for thirty-six holes. If we had two bags we were really worn down by the end of the day. But in our case, since we all had athletic ambitions, it helped our leg and shoulder muscles, and by the end of the summer we were ready for the football and basketball seasons.

There was a beach down below the caddy shack, and at the end of the day many of us would go there to swim, which was enjoyable after a day of caddying. Most of us learned to swim at Lake Tahoe.

One of the institutions at the Glenbrook golf course was Hughie O'Byrne, the clubhouse bartender. He was Irish to the core, had a heavy brogue, sort of a round and cherubic face, and white curly hair. He was so proud of his hair that he would gather rainwater to wash it—it was the only kind of water he would use. He was good to us guys. We were teenagers, and there was no chance he would give us even a taste of any alcoholic beverage.

I remember the Bliss family. Mr. Bliss would come out to the course occasionally, but not often. He was a friend of my father—my father was running sheep on Bliss property at Tahoe, so they had a relationship. In fact when I was going through my family things, I found a letter to my father from Mr. Bliss saying, "Yes, Dominique, I think we can find work for your oldest boys," and that is how we became caddies.

Mrs. Bliss poses an almost unforgettable picture in my mind. She was a quiet lady who was always so polite to us. When I would see her, she would have on a little sun-visor cap and would be sitting on the porch of one of the green cabins reading. If I were painting her, I would have named the painting "Woman in Repose."

In my mind the little green valley with its pine trees and story-book golf course seemed to have a mystical atmosphere. It was largely a family resort with many of the families coming back year after year. Most of them made reservations for the next season before they left, and some of them even asked for the same dining room table so that they could be with their friends at dinner.

With perhaps a few exceptions, the guests were ladies and gentlemen. Most of them were important people in their communities, but they were not the kind who flaunted their personal status.

Our caddy crew was sort of a mixture of personal backgrounds and our futures were to become quite diverse. Richard Jepson was on the *Enola Gay*, which dropped the first atom bomb; my brother Paul became governor of Nevada and U.S. senator; Bob Davenport served as clerk of the Nevada Supreme Court; and my other brothers, John and Peter, became successful lawyers. I cannot remember any Glenbrook caddies who didn't succeed in the work they chose. I think our characters were partly formed at Glenbrook. I think we learned to become gentlemen because we were with gentlemen—the quiet, civilized type of people of the world.

If all of the humorous anecdotes of happenings on the tricky Glenbrook course were compiled, a separate chapter probably would be required. Bill Bliss tells of a golfer who may have set some kind of a record for a slice off the first tee when his ball made a long loop and came back into the parking lot almost at right angles to the tee. He heard it hit something and, fearing it might have damaged one of the thirty-some cars parked there, he walked over to the lot to examine each of the vehicles with the hope of paying for any damage, if he could find the owner.

Locating the owner proved to be quite simple—his ball had broken the windshield of his own car.

Tennis champion Helen Wills Moody and fifteen-year-old Paul Laxalt prior to their match at Glenbrook in 1937.

One day Bob Laxalt caddied for a quiet, mild-mannered man who, on the first tee, sliced his ball far into the woods. On the second tee he hooked it into an unplayable lie in the rough. To shorten the story, not one of his tee shots landed on a fairway, and his iron shots were almost as bad.

After four putting the ninth green, he picked up his bag of clubs and walked to the nearest tree. He showed no sign of temper, but, as Bob stared open-mouthed, he systematically removed each club from his bag and, with a strong swing, wrapped it around the tree. When the bag was empty, he tipped Bob and walked to his car. Bob never saw him again.

Tennis was also a popular sport. In 1937 Helen Wills Moody was a guest at the Glenbrook Inn, where fifteen-year-old Paul Laxalt was working as a caddy. Laxalt, who was Nevada State Junior Tennis Champion that year, remembers the day Mrs. Moody invited him to play a match with her:

I was a young lad when word came that Helen Wills Moody was coming to Glenbrook to establish residence for a divorce. I was a caddy at that time.

Since I was heavily into tennis you can imagine how exciting it was to even have a chance to meet her since she was "it" as far as women's tennis was concerned.

When I was advised that she would not only meet me, but also would play tennis with me, I was thrilled and most apprehensive. I don't know who arranged the match, but I suspect that the Blisses and Charles Kitzmeyer from Carson, a tennis buff with a strong interest in me, must have arranged it.

As soon as I met her I was put completely at ease. She was a "queen" not only as a tennis player, but as a person. If I won a couple of games I'm sure it was due to her generosity, not my ability, because I wasn't anywhere in her league.

Thereafter, we worked out a few more times. Her advice and coaching were invaluable. My tennis improved immeasurably. I feel benefited to this day.

Of all the personages I've met over the years, I can't recall any that impressed me more or treated me more kindly under the circumstances.

Above all this was proof positive that America is truly a "land of opportunity." Where else would a sheepherder's son have a chance to play tennis with Mrs. Moody?

Sixteen :
The Final
Years

In 1947 Will Bliss's son Bill, having graduated from college and been discharged from the U.S. Navy, joined his father to assist in the management of the inn. A year later Doris Parriott was hired as secretary and before long became in many respects Glenbrook's key employee. No problem or complaint, whether a guest's or an employee's, was too small for her patience and understanding. Twenty-eight years later she was still solving minor and sometimes major problems.

Jack Morgan had become a fixture at the stable, and Ray Sendejas was becoming invaluable at the clubhouse bar. Ray, an excellent golfer, filled out many guest foursomes in the morning, quickly changing into a white jacket at noon and serving both partner and opponent. His bar was open evenings, and many guests of the inn

Will Bliss and Clark Gable *busing dishes at the Glenbrook Inn dining room after college student busboys had headed home for the fall semester.*

held their cocktail parties at what became informally known as Ray's Bar.

These employees and a number of others remained loyal to the Bliss family and to Glenbrook until the inn closed many years later. This loyalty, this lack of change in employees, lent a feeling of consistency—a serenity and security which guests could count on from year to year. This assurance was reflected in the large number of guests who returned summer after summer. To many it became a tradition—the last rite of a departing guest—to fill out a reservation form for the following year, which usually was a request for the same accommodations and comparable dates.

During its years of operation several well-known people were guests at the Glenbrook Inn. Clark Gable stayed there while establishing residency for a Nevada divorce. Actually, because of complications, he remained long after the inn closed that fall, taking care of his own room, eating with the caretakers while helping them drain the pipes and close the cottages along with all the other fall chores. He was entirely happy and contented with the simple existence. He lived there until sometime in December.

During subsequent seasons Gable would stop by to visit for a few days. His simplicity and friendship were indicated one evening in September when the dining room ran out of busboys, and Clark Gable joined Will Bliss to bus trays. It was quite an entertaining evening for the guests.

Rita Hayworth, also establishing residency for a divorce, stayed at Glenbrook during the same season Gable was there. Bill Bliss remembers:

She was a very simple, rather shy person who attempted to lead a quiet, normal life. She tried to avoid reporters except on a few occasions when she knew one of them had to get a story.

One day my sister and I had planned a cocktail party at our house, and during the late afternoon, while we were preparing hors d'oeuvres and setting up the bar on the kitchen sink, Rita Hayworth came by to help us. That evening Clark and I served drinks, and Rita stayed on along with many of our Glenbrook friends. It was a case of two very well-known people who thoroughly enjoyed the simple surroundings and circumstances and lack of special attention.

Clark was a good friend. The last time he stopped to visit he was finishing the filming of *The Misfits*. *1960*

Will Bliss died quite suddenly in February 1960 while he and the family and a number of friends were staying at Glenbrook while attending the Winter Olympics at Squaw Valley. Through his efforts the Glenbrook Inn had become a tightly knit organization. Overnight the responsibility to preserve it was passed on to his son.

Doris Parriott, Jack Morgan, and Ray Sendejas were invaluable. Don and Rose Corbin were employed as chef and dining room hostess, positions they held during the winter at Smoke Tree Ranch in Palm Springs. Glenbrook's reputation for excellent food continued. Joe and Mary Moniz took charge of the golf course pro shop, and Joe's reputation as a superb teaching professional drew golfers

Rita Hayworth comparing scores with Glenbrook golf pro Floyd Hudson.

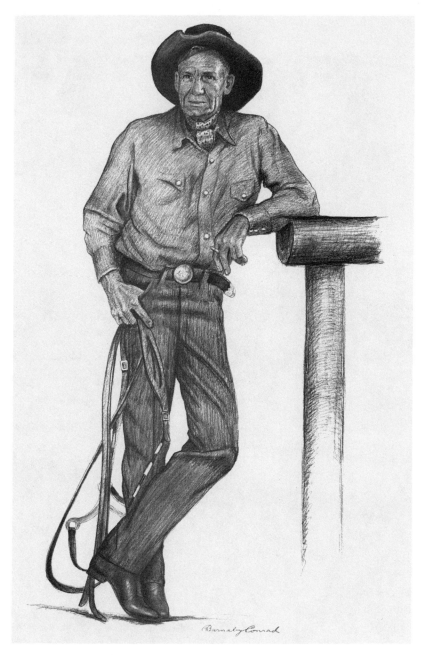

Jack Morgan, longtime Glenbrook wrangler. (Sketch by Barnaby Conrad)

from many areas. Longtime greens keeper Bill Beeson retired in his eighties, and Joe Rollino took over. These key employees remained through the summers of the 1960s and well into the 1970s.

Believing Will Bliss would have wished it, the rodeo was continued by his son and daughter, Bill and "Sis" Bliss, with the help of rancher Hap Magee. During those years a treasured belt buckle, in the name of Will Bliss, was awarded in team roping. To be eligible for the award—with the hope that winners would have known Will when he ran the show—the age of the two members of the victorious team had to total more than one hundred years. With a rare exception, the winners of the "Will Bliss Buckle" were old friends who had roped at Glenbrook for many years.

There was a respect and affection for Will Bliss that could not be properly described but which brought tears to the eyes of grown men who won the buckle and to many of those who missed winning it by a few fractions of a second.

Gradually, old-time summer resorts on Lake Tahoe were closing—the Tahoe Tavern in 1964 and Brockway in 1967. The reasons varied. Real estate developers converged on the lake in the 1960s, and with no practical building or planning restrictions, condominiums were built and sold by the hundreds. Motels, heretofore a rarity, sprang up along with many restaurants and dinner houses. Most, if not all, of the old Tahoe summer resorts operated on the American plan, the daily rate including three meals. With increasing opportunities for visitors to take some meals elsewhere, the American plan was gradually losing its appeal.

Perhaps the single most important factor in the loss of the old resorts was the increase in property values caused by development. Most resorts were not "winterized" and depended on a short summer season to make ends meet—which became increasingly impossible.

An article in the July 1967 issue of the periodical *San Francisco* stated:

Lake Tahoe certainly isn't the grand vacation spot it once was. The days of touring the waters by steam vessel, splendid dining, refined sport activities and Sunday promenades in elegant attire have long disappeared—probably never to return.

Of course, that was before the public even knew such a place existed. "Not everybody who came up here in the old days had money," said [a local man], "but they all loved Lake Tahoe for one reason or another. . . . and they weren't about to throw paper sacks in the water or leave beer cans along the beaches. . . . Soon as the real estate men and gamblers came along though, everything went to pieces."

Well, not exactly everything. There's still Glenbrook almost as it was in 1906 when the Bliss family converted part of their . . . lumber holdings into a resort. These days there are fourth generation families enjoying golf, swimming, boating, riding, hiking, dining and lodging at this untarnished bit of resort heaven.

Glenbrook could best be termed "comfortable, relaxed, friendly and simple," yet in no way should the description imply "ordinary." The operation is American Plan with three good meals per day. The quarters are situated in cabins—all with private bath. . . . most reservations are made for a week or longer. . . . By the way, no gambling here.

By not changing with the times, Glenbrook was becoming even more unusual—a loved, admired, reassuring oddity in a now rapidly changing environment. To the end, the Bliss family insisted on fresh table linen and bed linen daily, waitresses with starched aprons, and bus boys in immaculate white jackets (sometimes changed several times a day). Gentlemen guests were required to wear ties and coats at dinner.

But the problems which had closed the doors of other resorts eventually began seriously affecting the Glenbrook Inn. An agonizing decision was made by the Bliss family in late 1975; in January 1976 Bill Bliss mailed the following notice to hundreds of guests:

The Inn will not be open in 1976. The golf course, however, will be open.

The Nevada Industrial Commission requires us to totally rewire the Inn.

The Lake Tahoe Fire Protection District requires the same, in addition to major construction of additional exits and a totally new fire protection system.

Rudy, Billy, and Bill Bliss in front of Duane Bliss's summer home at Glenbrook. Billy is a member of the fifth generation of Blisses at Glenbrook. (Photo by Morton Beebe)

The Nevada State Department of Health code requires many costly additions to our kitchen.

The Environmental Protection Agency requires all facilities to be connected to the Tahoe Douglas Sewer District.

Financially, it is impossible to comply with the above.

The decision to discontinue operation of the Glenbrook Inn has been an extremely painful one.

An avalanche of letters from former guests arrived in short order, expressing dismay and disappointment, but at the same time, without exception, offering thanks and understanding. Several examples follow:

For one who has enjoyed Glenbrook since 1905, your note of Jan. 21, 1976 is very sad news. With deep gratitude for all your family has done for me and my family and friends, for some 70 years, I am with sincere thanks and good wishes, . . .

It was with such regret and sadness that I read the letter saying that the Inn was closing and permanently. I cannot imagine Tahoe without the Inn and the Bliss family. . . . my sympathy is enclosed for each and every one.

The wonderful memories of Glenbrook can't be dimmed and certainly never "discontinued" and I know that is the feeling of all those who received the painful news.

We've had so many good times there that we regard this as our personal loss.

We are grateful to have had the opportunity to share your gracious way of life with our children.

The closing of Glenbrook was like the passing of an old and beloved friend who was a mainstay, dependable and unchanging. When things became too frenetic at other times of year, one knew there would be that lovely peaceful time on the lake. . . . our whole family will always cherish the happy times we had at Glenbrook.

Perhaps the most succinct read:

Dear Bill,

This is a very sad day for all of us who loved Glenbrook, as well as for you. It is another example of the days of vanishing simple, wholesome pleasures. I am glad to have enjoyed it and seen it at its best.

Epilogue

The little valley has changed since 1975 when the Glenbrook Inn's last guest headed homeward. Where the forest prevented development, trees and other native vegetation have been thinned to allow space for access roads to homes, some of which are tucked into pleasant nooks of natural environment. Along the lakefront a section of the original town still stands. The inn, with its Lake Shore House and Jellerson Hotel additions, retains its charm as well as the atmosphere of comfortable relaxation it offered guests during its many years of operation.

A short distance north of the inn a small gully brings memories of the beautiful steamship *Tahoe,* for it was there that she was assembled and then allowed to slide down launching ways into the lake she would rule throughout her active life.

To a history-oriented visitor, the valley's old cemetery is of inter-

The meadow and buildings at Glenbrook, with Lake Tahoe and the Sierra in the background. (Julian P. Graham photo)

est. Protected by a white picket fence and scattered among tall and stately Jeffrey pine trees, grave markers of stone and weathered wood display the names of some of the early settlers. Fittingly, there is a large memorial monument for Duane L. Bliss, who might have wished for another marker beside it in memory of a man named "Diston."

Augustus Pray's grave is readily noticed. Perhaps fortuitously but certainly deservedly, it has one of the larger monuments—a tribute to an unusual and remarkable ship captain.

From the cemetery's higher elevation, one can still look down upon the untouched green meadow with bordering forest and, in the distance, make out the barn where dairy cows once provided fresh milk for inn guests. Nearby, the bleacher for the Will Bliss rodeo still stands.

And, if you have a true history buff's imagination, you can turn back the calendar over a hundred years to watch weary travelers in wagons or on foot passing by on the newly opened Lake Bigler toll road to Carson City and the Comstock. Some pause to purchase hay and vegetables, but they soon hurry on toward the mountain of silver and gold awaiting them.

And, regardless of the outcome, it seems certain that for many of them the journey will be, as it was for sixteen-year-old Duane Bliss, a great adventure.

Notes

Chapter 1: A Man Named Diston

1. William S. Bliss's five-page biographical sketch of his father, Duane L. Bliss, written for the family circa 1908.

2. Ibid.

3. W. S. Bliss's sketch provides only the name "Diston," apparently the man's surname.

4. Joseph Goldsborough, Bruff, *Gold Rush* (New York: Columbia University Press, 1949), p. 514.

5. David McCullough, *The Path Between the Seas* (New York: Simon and Schuster, 1977), pp. 33–40.

6. E. L. Autenrieth, *A Few Words for the Traveler over the Isthmus of Panama* (1851).

7. The American Medical Association, *Medical Encyclopedia* (New York: Random House, 1989) does not list a "Chagres Fever." It does list a Chagas Disease found in parts of South and Central America, caused by an infectious parasite. W. S. Bliss's sketch suggests Chagres Fever was "very likely typhoid or yellow fever." Malaria has also been suggested.

8. W. S. Bliss's sketch states that Duane Bliss "would have died had it not been for a professional gambler named Diston. Hundreds were dying of the fever when Diston, for six months, gave care and devotion to and risked his life for a stranger, a boy of sixteen."

9. W. S. Bliss: "On reaching San Francisco in the spring of 1850, Diston passed out of the picture, leaving no address and telling the youngster, 'I don't intend to have you follow my profession.'"

10. "However, they met on the street in Sacramento a short time after, and Diston again took the boy under his wing, going to the mines and leaving him in possession of a small but rich claim, admonishing him, at the time, to attend strictly to his work."

11. The piece of mining equipment called a "rocker" is a trough, usually four to six feet in length, with a series of cleats or riffles running crosswise along its slanting bottom. Suspended at the upper end of the trough, an open box with a sievelike bottom is filled with gold-bearing dirt over which water is poured. Particles small enough to pass through the perforated bottom are swept down the trough where the heavier pieces of metal, such as gold, become lodged behind the cleats or riffles. Material too large to pass through the holes in the box (hopper) is examined for large nuggets. The trough is supported by curved boards which allow it to be rocked from side to side to break up clumps of dirt. To catch even the smallest gold particles, mercury, which has an affinity for gold, is placed along the cleats or riffles where it amalgamates with the gold. To obtain the gold at the end of the working period, the amalgam is removed from the riffles and heated until the mercury vaporizes, leaving the gold behind. The mercury vapor is cooled to liquid form to be used again.

12. W. S. Bliss's sketch.

Chapter 2: Gold Hill, Nevada, 1863

1. Until the 1860s, there were no federal laws concerning the ownership of a mining claim on public lands. Miners formulated their own unofficial regulations, which became known as the "Miner's Code." J S. Holliday, *The World Rushed In* (New York: Simon and Schuster, 1981), p. 400.

2. Cecil G. Tilton, *William Chapman Ralston, Courageous Builder*, (Boston: Christopher Publishing House, 1935), p. 219.

3. J. Ross Browne, "A Peep at Washoe," first published in *Harper's New Monthly Magazine* (December 1861, January and February 1862; new printing; Palo Alto: Lewis Osborne, 1968), ch. 4, p. 79.

4. Age had made several of the words of the handwritten letter illegible by the time it was typed in 1949. However, it is certain that the few replacements have not altered the meaning.

5. "Square sets consist of short, square timbers, four to six feet long, mortised

and tenoned at the ends so they can be put together in a series of interlocked cribs and built up in a continuous row or block to any desired height or width, filling the whole chamber as fast as the ore is removed. By using diagonal braces, they could be indefinitely strengthened or made to fill a chamber of any shape. They can be framed together solidly, as is often done, so that the ore is replaced by a mass of lumber, or waste rock can be used so as to make solid pillars from floor to roof, or even fill the entire space." Charles Howard Shinn, *The Story of the Mine* (1910; reprint, Reno: University of Nevada Press, 1980), p. 96.

6. W. S. Bliss, sketch.

Chapter 3: Early Settler from Maine

1. Myron Angel, ed., *History of Nevada* (Oakland, Cal.: Thompson and West, 1881; reprint, Berkeley, Cal.: Howell-North, 1958), p. 541.

2. Ibid.

3. Andrew J. Marsh, *Letters from Nevada Territory, 1861–1862,* edited by William C. Miller, Russell W. McDonald, and Ann Rollins (Carson City: Legislative Counsel Bureau, State of Nevada, [1972]).

4. Edward B. Scott, *The Saga of Lake Tahoe,* 2 vols. (Crystal Bay, Nev.: Sierra-Tahoe Publishing Company, 1957), vol. 1.

5. Ralph Herbert Cross, "The Early Inns of California," (San Francisco: Cross and Brandt, 1954).

6. Scott, *The Saga of Lake Tahoe,* vol. 1.

7. Bliss family documents.

8. Alfred Doten, *The Journals of Alfred Doten, 1849–1903,* 3 vols., edited by Walter Van Tilburg Clark (Reno: University of Nevada Press, 1973), vol. 2, p. 1205.

9. Dan De Quille, *The Big Bonanza* (New York: Alfred A. Knopf, 1947), pp. 320–21.

10. Angel, *History of Nevada,* p. 381.

11. Ibid.

12. Scott, *The Saga of Lake Tahoe,* vol. 1.

13. Reverend A. H. Tevis, *Beyond the Sierras* (Philadelphia: Lippincott, 1877), pp. 143–44.

Chapter 4: Carson and Tahoe Lumber and Fluming Company

1. Tilton, *William Chapman Ralston.*

2. Shinn, *The Story of the Mine,* p. 242.

3. Angel, *History of Nevada,* p. 592.

4. Owen F. McKeon, "The Railroads and Steamers of Lake Tahoe," *Western Railroader* (March 1946), p. 5.

5. Ibid.

6. *New York Tribune,* September 16, 1875.

7. David F. Myrick, *Railroads of Nevada and Eastern California,* 2 vols. (Berkeley: Howell-North, 1962), vol. 1.

8. Scott, *The Saga of Lake Tahoe,* vol. 1, p. 171.

9. Bill Strobel, *Oakland Tribune,* December 18, 1961.

10. McKeon, "The Railroads and Steamers of Lake Tahoe," p. 9.

11. Scott, *The Saga of Lake Tahoe,* vol. 1, p. 289.

Chapter 5: A Box of Letters

1. *Carson City Appeal,* September 16, 1892.

2. Doten, *Journals,* vol. 3, p. 2104.

3. Bliss family papers.

4. The nationally known Mark L. Requa was born in Virginia City in 1865, the same year that his lifetime friend William S. Bliss was born in Gold Hill. Requa studied mining engineering in San Francisco under the direction of some of the leading mining men of the country. He practiced his profession in both Nevada and California and for a number of years was a member of the outstanding mining engineering firm of Bradley, Requa and Mackenzie. It was largely through his efforts that the Nevada Consolidated Copper Company was organized, and as general manager he built the Nevada Northern Railway. When his friend Herbert Hoover returned from Europe during World War I to become United States food administrator, he made Requa his assistant as fuel administrator. "Mark Requa," said Hoover, "was one of the most honest, the most loyal, the most idealistic men that California has produced." *Reno Evening Gazette,* March 6, 1937; *The National Cyclopaedia,* (New York: J. T. White, series 1898 to 1984), p. 472.

5. The buggy was an English surrey, probably a wedding present from Duane Bliss, Jr.

6. Coachella Valley is a large, arid region north of the Salton Sea. The discovery of underground water, supplemented in 1948 by the Coachella Canal bringing water from the All American Canal, brought irrigation to a portion of the valley. Truck crops, dates, citrus fruits, and alfalfa are grown in the region.

7. A U.S. Bureau of Mines Information Circular (February 1938) titled *Reconnaissance of Mining Districts in Humboldt County, Nevada,* by William O. Vanderburg, provides the following information: "Placer gold was discovered along Gold Run Creek in 1866, and the placers were worked in a desultory manner by small-scale sluicing and rocking for a number of years. . . . Accord-

ing to A. J. Landwith of Winnemucca, who has been familiar with mining activities in the district since 1890, the total placer production has been about $30,000." A notice of the appropriation of water and a claim on a water ditch leading from Rock Creek and its tributaries to Gold Run Creek Basin, in the handwriting of William Bliss but signed by his apparent partner, H. Warren, and recorded by the Humboldt county recorder on May 19, 1893, provide evidence that the Bliss project was placer mining.

8. T. R. Hofer, an original employee of the U.S. Mint in Carson City, worked his way up from a copying clerk in 1870 to superintendent in 1892. He held the position until May 20, 1894, when he was replaced by former governor Jewett W. Adams.

Chapter 6: Lake Tahoe Railway and Transportation Company

1. McKeon, "The Railroads and Steamers of Lake Tahoe" (p. 8), stated that the ship's speed was "18 ½ knots"—approximately 21.3 miles per hour.

2. See Ernest A. Lewis, *The Fremont Cannon, High Up and Far Back,* (Glendale, Cal.: Arthur H. Clark Company, 1981), chap. 5.

3. McKeon, "The Railroads and Steamers of Lake Tahoe," p. 8.

4. B.J.S. Cahill, "The Work of Bliss and Faville," *Architect and Engineer of California,* vol.35, No.3, January 1914.

Chapter 7: To Nome

1. Bliss family papers.

2. Myrick, *Railroads of Nevada,* vol. 1.

3. Francis Church Lincoln, "Some Economic Gold Deposits in Alaska," *Engineering and Mining Journal* (September 17, 1910).

4. Ibid.

5. Ibid.

6. Sally Carrighar, *Moonlight at Midday* (New York: Alfred A. Knopf, 1958).

7. Ibid.

8. Bliss family papers.

Chapter 8: Letters from Nome

1. Bliss family papers.

2. Lincoln, "Some Economic Gold Deposits in Alaska," p. 551.

3. S. F. Emmons and C. W. Hayes, *Contributions to Economic Geology,* U.S. Geological Survey, Bulletin No. 225 (1903), p. 49.

4. The archeologist's name for this throwing stick is "atlatl." It added velocity and distance to projectile shafts and was widely used throughout the Americas.

5. Mr. and Mrs. Harry Baldwin of Maui, Hawaii.

6. "Magar" was Will Bliss's name for his grandmother, Elizabeth Bliss.

Chapter 9: End of an Era

1. Bliss family papers.

2. This handwritten bill of sale, the only legal document required for sale of property, is in considerable contrast to today's requirements.

3. Bliss family papers.

4. McKeon, "The Railroads and Steamers of Lake Tahoe," p. 15.

Chapter 10: Tahoe Water

1. McKeon, "The Railroads and Steamers of Lake Tahoe."

2. Federal Water Master's Office, Reno, Nevada.

3. It is not certain whether Bliss removed the carburetor or the distributor—either would prevent the engine from operating.

4. Washoe Lake became entirely dry in 1934.

5. Letter from Carl Dodge, Jr., to the author.

6. Bliss family documents.

7. As members of the California-Nevada Interstate Compact Commission, later generations of the Bliss family accepted a share of the responsibility for the water of Lake Tahoe. Will M. Bliss was one of the original members of the commission; after his death, his son William W. Bliss represented Nevada.

Chapter 11: Time of Change

1. Bliss family.

2. McKeon, "The Railroads and Steamers of Lake Tahoe."

3. Scott, *The Saga of Lake Tahoe*, p. 407.

4. Ibid., p. 425.

5. Ibid., p. 434.

6. Charles T. Bliss worked in a management position at Hobart Mills, north of Truckee, for a number of years until 1910, when he took Duane's place as manager of Tahoe Tavern.

7. Duane L. Bliss, Jr., married Florence Dunham in 1910 and moved to San Francisco. He eventually became president of the wholesale hardware firm of

Dunham, Carrigan, and Hayden. The youngest of Duane L. Bliss's five children, he was the first to die.

8. During the early 1930s, when the author spent his summer college vacations working for the U.S. Forest Service, he met and talked to William S. Bliss several times. Bliss was a handsome man—tall, lean, and immaculately dressed. He was pleasant to the young college kid, who remembers thinking that the older man was the personification of a cultured gentleman.

Chapter 13: Fishing

1. By 1911 the outboard motor was available. It was named the Evinrude Detachable Row-Boat Motor.

2. W. H. Shebley, *History of Fishing and Fishing Conditions of Lake Tahoe, California* (Sacramento: California Division of Fish and Game, Bureau of Fish Culture, July 1929).

3. Richard Gordon Miller, "The Natural History of Lake Tahoe Fishes" (dissertation, School of Biological Sciences and Committee on Graduate Study of Stanford University, June 1951).

4. In the early days, until the 1960s, anglers occasionally caught a rare trout with external characteristics differing from Tahoe's native cutthroat or introduced rainbow. Because of its striking color and fighting qualities, for many years it was considered a prized catch by those fortunate enough to land one. Almo J. Cordone, fisheries management supervisor of the California Department of Fish and Game, provided me with the following information:

The royal silver trout was described as a full species (Salmo regalis) by ichthyologist, Dr. J. O. Snyder (1914). He felt it was a distinct and well-characterized species not closely related to either the cutthroat or rainbow trout. The description was based on three specimens, with color being the main criterion. . . . For many years, other ichthyologists concurred with Dr. Snyder, and their writings referred to the royal silver trout. . . .

In 1964 and 1965, we sampled the open waters of Lake Tahoe with monofilament gill nets. . . . Only 226 rainbow trout were caught in the pelagic [open water toward middle of lake] zone. . . .

I remember being very excited about the prospect of catching the mysterious royal silver trout. . . . Not surprisingly the trout taken from the pelagic zone were very silvery with some possessing the same attributes of the royal silver trout described by Snyder (1914, 1918): deep blue back, silvery sides, white belly, lack of spotting and loose scales. It was all very exciting until we noted that some of these fish were our marked hatchery reared trout planted as part of our experimental management program. Seventy-three of the total rainbow trout taken from open water were marked fish. . . .

Notes

Thus, what Snyder described as a unique species simply represents trout displaying an extreme form of silvery coloration associated with open water. Pelagic dwelling ocean fishes demonstrate the same phenomenon.

Chapter 14: Rodeos

1. During the times I talked to Will Bliss, he almost always wished to discuss the wildlife, especially the grouse, living in the mountains above Glenbrook. His interest in the outdoors was strong enough for him to be considered an amateur naturalist.

Index

Adams, Jewett W., 145n8
Alaska, 61–62, 70–78
All American Canal, 144n6
Automobile travel, 95, 97–98

Baer, Max, 123
Baker, W. H., 9
Baldwin, Harry, 73, 146n5
Baldwin, E. J. "Lucky," 52
Bank of California, 13–14
Barrett, Charles R., 16
Bates, Barbara, 98
Beatty, A. S., 16–18, 109
Beeson, Bill, 133
Benton's Stage Line, 19, 23
Bertolini, Louis, 121
Beyond the Sierras (Tevis), 22–23

Big Bonanza, The (De Quille), 19
Biltz, Norman, 105
Blasdel, Henry G., 18
Bliss, Billy, 135
Bliss, Charles Tobey, 14, 53, 98, 103, 146n6
Bliss, Duane C., xiii
Bliss, Duane Leroy: death, 84–85; and Diston, 2–6, 139; family homes, 47–48; Gold Hill years, 9–14; and Lake Tahoe water, 87; last trip, 81–84; mining claim, 5–6, 7–8, 142n10; South America voyage, 1–2; Western journey, 1, 2–6. *See also* Carson and Tahoe Lumber and Fluming Company; Lake Tahoe Railway and Transportation

Company; Tahoe Tavern

Bliss, Duane Leroy, Jr., 14, 40, 79, 82, 144n5; death, 103, 146–147n7; and Lake Tahoe Railway and Transportation Company, 53, 61; marriage, 146–147n7

Bliss, Elizabeth Tobey, 10–13, 75, 96, 98, 146n6

Bliss, Florence Dunham, 146n7

Bliss, Hatherly, 98, 105, 108, 116; "Sis," 133

Bliss, Hatherly Brittain, 98, 105, 115, 125

Bliss, Hope Danforth, 14, 40, 50, 53

Bliss, Lucia Mary, 1

Bliss, Mabel Williams, 39–46

Bliss, Rudy, 135

Bliss, Walter Danforth, 14, 48, 53, 79–80, 103; and Tahoe Tavern, 54–56, 98

Bliss, William, 1

Bliss, William Seth, 81–84, 102, 147n8; birth, 14; and Carson and Tahoe Lumber and Fluming Company, 86; death, 103; Gold Run Creek mine, 45, 60, 145n7; and Lake Tahoe Railway and Transportation Company, 53–54, 60–61, 86, 97, 98–99; and Lake Tahoe water projects, 89–93, 103, 146n3; marriage, 39–46, 144n5; Nome mining operation, 71–78; and steamships, 100, 101; voyage to Nome, 61–70

Bliss, William W. "Bill," 102, 105, 128, 130, 133, 134, 135; as golf caddy, 108, 121; Inn closing, xiv, 134, 136; and Lake Tahoe water, 146n7

Bliss, Will M., 47, 98, 102, 130; and Depression, 103; and Glenbrook Inn, 104–106, 107–108, 124–125; and Lake Tahoe water, 146n7; and

rodeos, 114, 115, 116–117, 118, 133; and *Tahoe* launching, 50; and Tahoe Tavern, 98

Bliss and Faville, 98, 103

Bliss Mansion, 47

Bonner, Charles, 18

Bourne, A. K., 124

Brittain, Hatherly. *See* Bliss, Hatherly Brittain

Brockway, 133

Brodell, Arthur D., 99

Browne, J. Ross, 9–10

Brynteson, J. J., 62

Buggy Ride to Tahoe, A (Estudillo), 17

Bulger, John, 50

Byron, M., 81

Caldwell, Mr., 18

California-Nevada Interstate Compact Commission, 146n7

Carson and Tahoe Lumber and Fluming Company, 14, 26–38; conservation, 37–38; flumes, 30, 31–34; property sales, 105; railways, 34–36, 52–53; sawmills, 29, 30–31

Carson City Daily Appeal, 84

Carson City Morning Appeal, 43–45

Carson City News, 49

Center, Samuel, 81

Central Pacific Railroad, 87

Chagres Fever, 3–4, 141n7, 142n8

Childers, A., 21–22

Chinese population, 29

Coachella Valley, 45, 144n6

Cobb, W. A. B., 22

Colbath, Lou L., 16

Comstock, H. O., 52

Conservation, 37–38

Corbin, Don, 130

Corbin, Rose, 130

Couillard, D., 80

Crown Point mine fire, 27, 28

Daniel, William T. "Bill," 111–113
Davenport, Bob, 125
Deep Well Guest Ranch, 106
Deidesheimer, Philipp, 13
Deleray, Mr., 72, 74
Depression (1930s), 103
De Quille, Dan, 19–20
Diston, 2–6, 139, 142nn8, 9, 10
D. L. Bliss State Park, xiii, 37
Dodge, Carl F., Jr., 91
Dodge Construction, Inc., 91
Dohrmann, Bruce, 99
Donner Lumber and Fluming Company, 88
Doten, Alfred, 19
Drum, John, 99
Dunham, Carrigan and Hayden, 146–147n7
Dunham, Florence. *See* Bliss, Florence Dunham

Emerald Number One (ship), 30
Emerald Number Two (ship), 30, 52
Emmons, Hank, 106, 110
Esberg, Milton, 99
Estudillo, Jesus Maria, 17

Fair, James, 32–34
Faville, William B., 54–56, 98, 103
Fishing, 95, 109–113, 147–148nn1, 4
Fleischmann, Max C., 105, 124
Fleishacker, Herbert, 99
Flood, James, 32
Flumes, 30, 31–34
Fonda, Mr., 18
Foote, Billy, 110
Forsythe, Robert, 50

Gable, Clark, 129–130
Gardner, Matthew Culbertson, 34–35
Glenbrook Hotel Company, 18

Glenbrook (Glen Brook) House, 16, 16–18, 18–20, 109
Glenbrook Improvement Company, 79, 83–84. *See also* Glenbrook Inn
Glenbrook Inn, 139; and Depression, 101, 103; design of, 79–81; employees, 106–107, 108, 128–129, 130, 132, 133; famous guests, 129–130, 131; final days, xiv, 133–137; fishing, 109–113; golf and tennis, 106, 119–127; improvements, 103, 104, 105–106; present site, 138–140; rodeos, 114–118, 133, 140; success of, 94–95, 101, 106; travel to, 95, 97–98; and World War II, 107–108
Glenbrook Inn and Ranch, 106. *See also* Glenbrook Inn
Glenbrook (Nevada), 14, 18; early settlement, 15–16; growth, 36; Pray's development, 20–25, 29. *See also* Glenbrook Inn
Gold Hill, 9–14
Gold Hill Bank, 9, 13–14
Gold Hill News, 19
Gold Run Creek mine, 45, 60, 144–145n7
Golf Digest, 119
Governor Blasdel (ship), 21
Grant, Ulysses S., 18
Greeley, Horace, 19
Greig, James, 51

Haley, J. V., 79
Ham, William, 100, 101
Harte, Bret, 18
Hayward, Alvinza, 27
Hayworth, Rita, 130, 131
Henderson, D. M., 81
Henningson, C. C., 97
Hitchcock, Lillie, 19
Hobart, William Scott, 101
Hobart Mills, 146n6

Hofer, T. R., 45, 145n8
Hogan, Ben, 119, 121
Hollister, Graham, 116
Hoover, Herbert, 144n4
Hudson, Floyd, 121, 131
Hummel, John, 62

Ickcs, Harold, 91–92
Imelli, Allie, 106, 114
"Indian Mattie," 106

James, Harry, 110
Jeannie (ship), 63–70
Jellerson Hotel, 138
Jepson, Richard, 125
Jones, John P., 9, 27–28

Kent, William, 88
Kentuck Mine, 27
Kitzmeyer, Charles, 127

Lake Bigler toll road, 16, 140
Lake Shore House, 22, 80, 138, 139,
   146n2
Lake Tahoe: map, xvi; water projects,
   86–93, 103, 146nn3, 4, 7
Lake Tahoe Railroad, 34, 36
Lake Tahoe Railway and Transporta-
   tion Company: creation, 53–54,
   60–61; finances, 82; sale, 97, 98–
   99; trips on, 56–57, 95
Lake Tahoe Transportation Com-
   pany, 48–53, 53
Lake Tahoe Water Conference Com-
   mittee, 91
Landwith, A. J., 145n7
Laxalt, John, 125
Laxalt, Paul, 125, 126, 127
Laxalt, Peter, 125
Laxalt, Robert, 122–125, 126
Linnard Hotel, 99
Lombard, Carole, 98
Louis, Joe, 123–124

McDowell, Irvin, 18
Mackay, John, 32, 85
McKeon, Owen, 32
Magee, Hap, 133
Marion B (boat), 99
Matthewson, Capt., 50
Meteor (ship), 29–30, 52, 100
Miller, Joaquin, 19
Mills, Darius Ogden, 14, 27, 85
Mining, xiii; Duane L. Bliss's claim,
   5–6, 7–8, 142n10; equipment, 6,
   142n11; Gold Run Creek, 45, 144–
   145n7; "Miner's Code," 8, 142n1;
   Snake River strike, 61–62; timber-
   ing methods, 13, 142–143n5;
   William Bliss's Nome operation,
   70–78; Yellow Jacket mine fire,
   27–28
Mogenberg, Mrs., 18
Moniz, Joe, 121, 130, 133
Moniz, Mary, 130
Monk, Hank, 19–20, 22
Moody, Helen Wills, 126, 127
Moran, Molly, 110
Morgan, Jack, 117–118, 128, 130,
   132
Mullins, Ella, 106
Murdock, N. E., 15–16

Nevada (ship), 52, 54, 83, 100
Nevada Consolidated Copper Com-
   pany, 144n4
Nichols, Tom, 106, 121
Nye, James W., 18

O'Brien, William, 32
O'Byrne, Hughie, 124
Ophir Company, 13

Pacific Wood, Lumber, and Fluming
   Company, 32
Parriott, Doris, 130
Paul, Almarin B., 9

Pinchot, Gifford, 88
Pomin, Ernest John, 79, 80, 82
Pray, Capt. Augustus W., 15, 16, 20–25, 29, 80, 139

Ralston, William, 18, 27
Ramsdell, H. J., 32–34
Reclamation Act (1902), 87
"Report—On the Lake Tahoe-Truckee River and Carson Rivers Water Situation" (Bliss), 92
Requa, Mark L., 42, 45, 60, 144n4
Rigby, James A., 14, 21
Riverside (California) *Daily Press*, 84–85
Roads, 95, 97–98
Rodeos, 114–118, 133, 140
Rollino, Joe, 133

San Francisco, 133–134
San Francisco Call Bulletin, 107
San Francisco Chronicle, 85
Saxon, Lloyd, 101
Saxton, Augustus, 18
Schneider, Frank, 106–107
Seitz, Nick, 119
Sendejas, Ray, 128–129, 130
Shannon, Fay, 105, 107
Sharon, William, 14, 18, 27, 85
Sheridan, Philip H., 18
Short, F. R., 81
Southern Pacific Company, 99
Square set timbers, 13, 142–143n5
Stanford, Leland, 19
Steam vessels, 20–21, 48; Carson and Tahoe Lumber and Fluming Company, 29–30; sinking of, 99–101. *See also specific ships*
Stewart, William M., 18
Stone and Webster, 88–89
Summer homes, 104–105, 138
Sutherland, William, 22

Taft, William Howard, 88
Tahoe (ship), 48–53, 54, 82, 95, 100–101, 138
Tahoe Tavern, 98, 99, 133, 146n6; design, 54–56; success, 57–59, 82; travel to, 56–57
Tallac (ship), 48, 52
Temperance, 24–25
Tevis, A. H., 22–23
Tevis, William S., 87
Titus, Frank, 82
Tobey, Ada, 51
Tobey, Elizabeth T. *See* Bliss, Elizabeth Tobey
Tobey, Walter D., 53
Truckee-Carson Irrigation District, 87, 91
Truckee General Electric Company, 88–89
Truckee Lumber Company, 54
Truckee Meadows Conservation District, 89

U.S. Department of the Interior, 88, 89
U.S. Reclamation Service, 87, 88–89, 90, 91

Vance, Johnny, 114, 117
Vesey, Horace M., 18
Virginia City Territorial Enterprise, 19, 24, 25
Von Schmidt, A. W., 87

Walton, Rufus, 15–16
Warren, G. W., 15–16
Warren, H., 145n7
Washoe Conservation District, 91–92
Watkins, Carleton E., 18
Welton, W. B., 22
West, Frazer, 116
Whittell, "Captain" George, 105

"Will Bliss Buckle," 133
Williams, Mabel. *See* Bliss, Mabel
  Williams
Winters, Joseph D., 16
Wonders of Nevada, The (Sutherland),
  22

World War II, 107–108

Yellow Jacket mine fire, 27–28
Yerington, Bliss, and Co., 14
Yerington, Henry Marvin, 14, 26–27,
  84